ELEMENTS OF RELIGION

ELEMENTS OF RELIGION

BY HENRY EYSTER JACOBS

EDITED BY JORDAN COOPER

JUST AND SINNER PUBLICATIONS
FAIRFIELD, IA 2013

CONTENTS

INTRODUCTION 9

PREFACE 11

PART I: PREREQUISITES OF REDEMPTION 15

CHAPTER 1: THEOLOGY AND REDEMPTION 17

CHAPTER 2: THE HOLY SCRIPTURES 27

CHAPTER 3: GOD 37

CHAPTER 4: GOD AS CREATOR: ANGELS 49

CHAPTER 5: GOD AS CREATOR: MAN 53

CHAPTER 6: SIN 57

CHAPTER 7: WAGES OF SIN 63

PART II: PREPARATION OF REDEMPTION 67

CHAPTER 8: THE GROUND AND GOAL OF REDEMPTION 69

CHAPTER 9: GOD'S ETERNAL PURPOSE 73

CHAPTER 10: PROVIDENCE AND ITS RELATION TO REDEMPTION 79

CHAPTER 11: ONE PERSON AND TWO NATURES 89

CHAPTER 12: THE HUMILIATION 95

CHAPTER 13: THE EXALTATION 111

CHAPTER 14: THE OFFICES OF CHRIST 123

CHAPTER 15: THE KINGDOM OF GOD   123

PART III: THE APPLICATION OF REDEMPTION   129

CHAPTER 16: THE DISPENSATION OF THE HOLY SPIRIT   131

CHAPTER 17: THE WORD   137

CHAPTER 18: LAW AND GOSPEL   149

CHAPTER 19: WORD AND SACRAMENTS   153

CHAPTER 20: THE WORD AND PRAYER   165

PART IV: THE EFFECTS OF REDEMPTION   167

CHAPTER 21: REGENERATION   169

CHAPTER 22: FAITH   175

CHAPTER 23: FAITH OF INFANTS   183

CHAPTER 24: JUSTIFICATION   189

CHAPTER 25: SANCTIFICATION   199

CHAPTER 26: GOOD WORKS   205

CHAPTER 27: GLORIFICATION   211

PART IV: THE ADMINISTRATION OF REDEMPTION   219

CHAPTER 28: THE CHURCH   221

CHAPTER 29: THE MINISTRY   231

INTRODUCTION

HENRY Eyster Jacobs was one of the most important voices of 19th century American Lutheranism. He was born in 1844 in Gettysburg, Pennsylvania, and attended the Lutheran Seminary in that town. He taught systematic theology at Pennsylvania College and later at the Lutheran Theological Seminary of Mt. Airy. He later became the Dean and President of the Mt. Airy Seminary. He died in 1932.

Jacobs provided many essential English resources to the Lutheran church in America. He translated several Lutheran Dogmatics works for use at seminaries, and wrote two different Dogmatics textbooks himself, including the present work. He was the chief editor of the multivolume *Lutheran Commentary* series, which collected exegetical treatments of the Biblical books from the best Lutheran scholars of the 19th and 20th centuries. He also published the often referenced *Lutheran Cyclopedia* in 1899. Among his own works are a biography of Martin Luther, commentaries on Romans, Galatians, and 1 & 2 Corinthians, and studies on Lutheran influence on the Anglican Church.

Of Jacobs' two Dogmatics texts, the present one is the shorter treatment of theology. The previous English

Dogmatics handbooks were translations of German volumes; this was the first written in English specifically for the American church. Jacobs basically follows the traditional *Loci* method of Lutheran scholasticism, without deviating from the Dogmatic tradition on any major point. His work thus functions as a summary of the German theological tradition in the post-Reformation era.

Jacobs' work serves as a summary rather than extended defense of Lutheran doctrine. He covers all major points of Christian theology including the doctrine of God, salvation, the sacraments, Christ, and the church. He writes with both brevity and clarity, making this an ideal guidebook for those who are interested in beginning a study of the Lutheran theological tradition. Where possible, Jacobs gives Biblical and historical defenses of his positions, and does so convincingly.

This works serves as an introduction to Jacobs' theology, while his other Dogmatics text, *A Summary of the Christian Faith*, published ten years later, gives a more extended treatment of Christian theology. The latter volume discusses Dogmatics in a question and answer format, whereas the present work engages in a more traditional *Loci* format. The later volume will be published later in the present series, and will serve to expound upon the themes introduced in the present text.

There has not been a significant amount of editing in this work, as Jacobs' writing is extremely lucid and straightforward. He avoids technical theological terminology where possible, and where it is used he explains his terminology. There were occasional changes of words and sentence structure to allow for easier reading, but the present text is almost identical to the original.

Jordan Cooper
2013

PREFACE

Some time ago, two clergymen, writing without consultation, from different parts of the country, almost simultaneously requested us to prepare a volume of essays on Doctrinal Theology, adapted to the wants of inquirers, both within and without the communion to which we belong. It was represented that, in these times of unrest and subtle skepticism, there was a call for a treatment of theological questions in a plain, direct and straightforward way, avoiding the technicalities of professed scientific expositions, and better adapted to our age and country, than the translations of excellent works that have proved of great service to many among us.

The author, who has for some years been endeavoring to teach Theology, recognized in the suggestion an opportunity to present, in a familiar and connected form, his own personal testimony on topics, the significance and life of which, he has often apprehended, are obscured by the close methods of analysis and demands of rigid, logical precision necessarily required in their more scientific treatment. His highest delight in the class room has been whenever he could push aside text-book and lecture, and could speak from his own convictions on these living topics. Nor has he ever found his students un-responsive when such liberty to depart from the prescribed routine was taken. In this book he has endeavored to write with similar freedom. The book was written amidst the duties of session time, under the stimulus of daily contact with students in the class-room, and with their many questions and perplexities in view. The fruits of the author's reading throughout his entire life have been ever in mind; but, as a rule, he has ventured to write without accumulating authorities. The aim is to present, in a plain form, a restatement of the main argument of revealed religion. He has hoped in this way to aid students in unifying the knowledge, which, in such an indispensable work as Schmid's *Doctrinal Theology, of the Evangelical Lutheran Church*, is presented in a very fragmentary way that often confuses one who attempts to study it consecutively. In the arrangement of his material, he has neither endeavored to conform to previous writers, nor to depart from them. He does not offer his construction of the system as the best attainable, or as a great improvement on those that have already been given; but he hopes that some of the doctrines in the true, although not very usually assigned relations in which they are placed, may gain fresh interest.

The author is a Lutheran, who, without being blind to the great merits and distinguished services of theologians of other Churches, accepts, with ever increasing devotion, the matchless expositions of Scriptural truth contained in the Lutheran Confessions. He recognizes, however, the fact that the Church of every age and every land has a peculiar calling to fulfill and a peculiar service, in the development of the kingdom of God, to perform. To confess the same faith in many lands and many tongues requires more than the translation of the same treatise from one language into the others. As with our sermons, so it must also be with our theology; we cannot depend upon translations, except as merely temporary expedients. The matter remains permanent; but the form changes not only with the language, but with the age, the currents of thought and the diverse classes of errors and attacks that succeed one another with great rapidity. We must speak the language of the time and place where Providence has placed us.

The reference to authorities generally excluded in the text, for the purpose of avoiding a break in the argument, has been at least partially supplied by an appendix. We hope that the illustrative matter, there found, may be serviceable to Chaptthose who desire a fuller and more thorough treatment. Much has been included that has been profitable and interesting to the author, and which he believes will be valuable to his readers. Not the least important are testimonials to the force of the Lutheran position by theologians of other communions. Several questions of interest have also been presented there more fully than was possible in the text, where it has been our purpose to exhibit results rather than processes.

Henry E. Jacobs
Mt. Airy, Philadelphia
Aug. 15th, 1894

PART I

THE PRE-REQUISITES OF REDEMPTION

CHAPTER I
THEOLOGY AND RELIGION

THEOLOGY is the science which treats of the revelation of God to man. It presupposes that there is a God, that He has made a revelation, and that, however inexplicable be the mysteries connected with this revelation, all that is comprised therein may be known. We know God, so far as He has given us capacities to know Him, and has enabled us to exercise these capacities upon the truths that He communicates to us.

When Theology is defined, as the science of religion, no contradiction with the above definition is involved, but reference is had to the fact that all revelation has a practical end. God's revelation of Himself to man is for the purpose of implanting and developing within man a new life. By the study of this new life, which is the result of the presence of God's Spirit within man, and which is constantly unfolding itself in the lives of individuals and the life of the Church, we trace more and more the details of God's revelation. Theology, thus considered, is not occupied with what God is apart from His relations to man, but with what He is in and through and for these relations.

What, then, is religion? It is the communion of man with God. It affirms not only the possibility, but also the reality of a life of man in God, and a life of God in man. God and man are forever distinct. There are two personalities, one infinite and the other finite, bound together by the closest union, so that the finite is made partaker of the resources of the infinite. It is the office of the science of religion to teach us who these persons are, whence this communion comes, what it is and whither it tends. It gathers together and presents in order all the teachings of revelation concerning what man is towards God, and what God is towards man. But since what God is to man and what man is to God in this communion is realized only in the Christian life, theology, as the science of religion, may be defined, as the science of the Christian life.

Religion comes to man through the revelation to him of God's love. Man enters into communion with God by learning what God's love towards him is. But he learns this, only as God declares and unfolds it. He knows nothing, and can know nothing of God, except what God Himself discloses. God reveals Himself in Nature; and this revelation in Nature is described in Psalm 19:1; Acts 17:24-26; Romans 1:18. But this is insufficient to bring about a life-communion between man and God. It is, on the one hand, a revelation of wrath, Romans 1:18. It is, on the other, only a suggestion of a clearer and fuller revelation that is to follow, Acts 17:23. It is a voice of God, asserting His supreme claims to man's love and worship, Romans 2:15; but bringing no answer to the question as to how such love and worship are to be rendered. It keeps man from being completely absorbed in the life of Nature, by ever reminding him of what is beyond and above Nature. The various false religions derive whatever elements of strength they have solely from this natural revelation. It asserts that there is a God, but fails to declare who or what God is. Some of His attributes are made manifest; but all foundation for the reconciliation and the intimate union between man and God is lacking. Either some of the features of the primitive revelation of God, preserved by tradition from a purer period, are perverted, distorted and unduly emphasized by the loss of other doctrines, or the human mind, by the contemplation of Nature, and, by reflection upon itself, rising from the feeblest apprehensions of a higher power, like one—to use a figure of Tertullian—awakening from the stupor of intoxication, gropes painfully amidst the thick darkness towards the glow of coming day.

If man is ever to have communion with God, this feeble light of Nature, that comes only like the faint streaks of early dawn, must be lost in the clear and full exhibition of what God is to us in Christ. We know God only as the Son of God has declared him, John 1:18. As natural revelation, or the revelation of Creation, teaches us that there is a God, supernatural revelation, or the revelation of Redemption, teaches who and what God is. The religion which comes from natural revelation goes no farther than to seek after God; the only true religion is that in which the revelation of God is so certain and distinct, that man can live in the consciousness of God's presence and favor, of God's direction and support and omnipotent efficiency.

This supernatural revelation of God has its degrees, as it progressively unfolds itself through all the stages of the world's history. When it is said that God is known only in Christ, by this we do not mean that the knowledge of what God is in Christ was entirely withheld until the incarnation of the Son of God. As the eternal, personal Word, he was in all ages the great Revealer. The revelation of Redemption began immediately after man's fall; at first indistinctly and faintly, but growing in brightness with every succeeding era, until at last when Christ came, the mystery hidden from the ages became manifest—Col. 1:26; Eph. 3:9. Even the lower degrees of this revelation called forth and sustained and developed a religious life in man, as plants may grow and bloom in a cell into which only a few rays of light fall. Enough truth was given to assure man that God is both just and merciful, and, by the assurance of God's love to the sinful, to bring man to God, and to enable him to look forward into the future for some signal display of Divine mercy, he could not tell what or how, whereby his complete deliverance from sin and highest enjoyment of God would be obtained. Thus the communion of God with man was restored in the first years of the human race. Men walked with God. They knew God as an ever living, ever loving, ever present personality, the one great reality to them beneath all other realities, nearer and more accessible than anything that they could see or hear. They knew that wherever they went God went, and wherever they were God was, and however alone they might seem in the silence of the night, or the seclusion of the desert, God always talked with them and they with God. From this communion with God, they ever drew new strength for the performance of life's duties and the endurance of life's trials. If they had put into writing all that they knew of God and their relations to Him, and their experience of His loving favor, this would have been a theology of the patriarchal age.

But, with all this, they carried with them the sense of the incompleteness of this communion. They ever longed to be nearer to God, to know more of the mysteries of His love and wisdom, to be more wholly devoted to His will. Their communion with Him was mingled with overwhelming disclosures of their sinfulness and unworthiness. There was something distant and external about their relation. There were seeming contradictions in their experience that they could not reconcile. Even when they knew Him to be nearest, He seemed to them to be most remote. Even when they were sure of His constant presence, He seemed to appear and to speak only at intervals, and only a small portion of His will concerning them, withholding freedom of utterance, like one whose confidence has been only partially gained. Jacob's wrestling with the angel, Gen. 32:24-30, tells the whole story. The "divers portions" and "divers manners" of the Old Testament pointed towards a more direct and consoling expression of God's will, to be found in the unity and permanency of a higher revelation and still closer communion with man, Heb. 1:1-2.

In the Old Testament there was progress, both in revelation and in man's apprehension of the con tents of this revelation. To Abraham God revealed Himself more fully than to Adam, to Moses more fully than to Abraham, to David more fully than to Moses, to Isaiah more fully than to David. The faces of all are turned towards a future, ever brightening as the centuries advance. But there was progress also in man's apprehension of the contents of revelation. It is not on the first reception of a word of God, that its meaning is most clearly understood. The word must enter the life and develop there its spiritual capacities. The appropriation and assimilation of the word is gradual, day after day, and year after year of the religious life, affording ever new occasions for its application, and new relations in which its precious powers are exercised. While the individual thus grows in his personal apprehension of the contents of the revelation which he has long possessed, the fruits of his experience are transmitted to those who succeed him. The religious experience of one generation becomes the heritage of the possessors of the same religious life in the next generation. This is the meaning of the words: "I am the God of Abraham and of Isaac and of Jacob," Matt. 22:32. The Old Testament saints were not, therefore, confined to the knowledge of the mere words in which God had declared to them His will, but each one, looking back upon his own life, and upon that of those who preceded him, could read the Word as interpreted, by numberless incidents of human experience in divine things. Not that experience is in any way the test of truth, but that the Word as the constant test of experience, manifests, through this process, resources which at first were unthought of.

As the knowledge of God, communicated through revelation and constantly more fully apprehended in human experience, was unfolded, it found its record in the successive books of the Old Testament, written under inspiration of the Holy Spirit.

The Old Testament revelation was, however, only a feeble light, when compared with that of the New Testament. The fullness of God's revelation entered, when God took humanity into personal union with Himself. When "the Word was made flesh and dwelt among us," John 1:14; they who saw Him saw the Father, John 14:9. This made the greatest under the Old Testament, less than the least under the New, Matt. 11:11. In Christ, man's longing for complete union and reconciliation with God, and with it, the satisfying of the desire for knowing God, was at last to be accomplished. But here again, this knowledge was attained only gradually. The Lord of Glory, incarnate in weak humanity, leads His people by slow stages to the understanding of what He is and whence and for what He comes. The story of that wonderful earthly life is a succession of revelations and surprises. Every descent into a valley of humiliation, is only a preparation for an ascent to an elevation far beyond what had been previously reached. The dark shadows of the valley of Gethsemane lead to Olivet and the higher glories beyond. He reveals Himself both in holy deeds and in words of saving power, forever impressed upon the minds of those who are with Him, even though they understand but little of their deep significance. The disciples were like collectors of a vast literature written in hieroglyphics that must be deciphered in coming years, on a distant shore and by long practice. So the words were gathered to be recorded and applied only when the promise would be fulfilled: "The Holy Ghost shall bring all things to your remembrance, whatsoever I have said unto you," John 14:26. To use another figure, the negative was photographed when the Lord was present to their sight; but the development of that impression continues through the power of the Holy Spirit throughout succeeding ages.

None were more conscious of this process, and how far they were from attaining perfection in apprehending the contents of revealed truth, than those who made the greatest progress in this sphere. Paul confesses that the love of Christ passes knowledge, Eph. 4:19. All truth was given in Christ. Nothing remained to be said concerning the will of God towards man. In Him revelation was complete. The one complete revelation in Christ is contrasted with the many partial revelations of a former period, Heb. 1:1-2. But the contents of this one revelation are more and more unfolded and applied under the leading of the Spirit, until the highest stage of revelation is reached in the world to come, where we will no longer know in part, but as we are known, 1 Cor. 13:12.

This process may be traced in the New Testament Canon. The last of the Gospels excels, in depth and inwardness, those that precede it, to such a degree that the distinction between the Synoptics and the Gospel of John is one of the most prominent features of New Testament study. The Epistles are explanations, defenses and applications of the doctrine of Christ, made, as the Holy Spirit brought His teachings to mind, and preserved the writers from error in representing and recording them.

But the process did not cease with the completion of the New Testament Canon and the days of inspiration. The Holy Spirit came to God's people on the Day of Pentecost, to abide with them forever, John 14:16. He is no less present in the Church of the Nineteenth, than He was in the Church of the First Century. Under His leading and inner impulse, believing men have been ever brought to a clearer and fuller apprehension of the doctrines given once for all in Holy Scripture. All the products of this working of the Holy Spirit in the experience of the Church are to be carefully treasured and to be thankfully used. The Holy Scriptures afford the test whereby to discriminate a true from a false development. All that is not contrary to Holy Scripture in the life of the Church belongs to the providential development of its capacities, as the witness of the truth and the bearer of salvation. Well-known as may be a passage or a series of passages of Scripture and abundant in consolation, a joyful discovery of riches previously not thought of hidden therein, often follows, when error seeks to pervert it; and the confusion which is threatened, forces the individual Christian, or a Church communion to its most thorough study. For a time, the violence of controversy may be heard, and the fact be deeply deplored that Christian men instead of applying the word of Scripture to the wants of practical life, should allow their energies to be dissipated by polemical zeal. But the rise of every error and the rage of every controversy point to an ultimate victory. Men are forced anew to the Word of God; arguments on the one side and on the other, are carefully balanced, the ardor of contestants only contributing more fully to the wealth of material that is gathered, and the wider outlook which the controverted passage or doctrine opens. The result is the formulation of a definition or statement, condensing declarations found in numerous Scriptural passages, and expressed in language so thoroughly guarded as to exclude the errors which threatened to enter under the garb of more general terms that had hitherto been used. Such a definition settling a controversy, and officially approved as a test of sound teaching, is called a dogma.

The dogmas, or officially approved definitions, of the Church are set forth in the Church's Confessions of Faith. They have their authority not from the Church, but from their agreement with Holy Scripture. A pure dogma, therefore, combines two elements: Its material is from the Holy Scriptures; its form has been determined by the Church's experience. It has, therefore, both a Scriptural and an historical side.

The science which exhibits the dogmas of the Church in their connection is the science of Dogmatics. The distinction between Biblical Theology and Dogmatics can be clearly drawn. Biblical Theology ignores all other sources but the Bible. Dogmatics uses as its sources the Bible and the results of the Church's experience as expressed in definitions, whose truth can be proved from the Bible. Dogmatics proceeds even further. It may use the results attained by the experience of the Church and the individual believer in the application and defense of the Church's dogma.

Regarding, then, theology as the science of religion, and religion as the communion of man with God, a correct dogmatic method investigates the principles from which this communion comes, and by which it is supported and developed. But its sphere cannot be limited to the consideration of those truths which belong to the individual's personal experience of God's saving grace. It includes all that is contained in Holy Scripture, whether this can be traced in human experience or not. Its sphere comprehends that of Biblical Theology, as well as that of the Church's dogmas. Thus, while our own experience, and the experience of the Church for ages give us no data for a dogma concerning angels, yet as the Holy Scriptures teach their existence and offices, the theologian must believingly appropriate, state and defend all that Scripture says concerning them. But on the doc trines of sin, the need of redemption, and the applying grace of the Holy Spirit, Christian experience most abundantly illustrates the statements of Holy Scripture, and hence enters as a most important factor for an adequate treatment.

CHAPTER II
THE HOLY SCRIPTURES

THE Holy Scriptures are the infallible and inerrant record of God's revelation of His saving grace to men. Since the revelation was made long before it was committed to writing, the record is not the sole source of the truths which it contains. The first source of the New Testament message was the oral communication of this revelation by Christ and his Apostles. As it is not the record, but the truth borne by the record, which is the organ of the regenerating and converting influences of the Holy Spirit, this same truth orally communicated in Apostolic days and since then, is just as efficient as when it is read from the pages of Scripture. But while the statement that the Holy Scriptures are the sole source of revealed truth requires this qualification, they are to be revered as the chosen means for preserving the purity of the Apostolic teaching, since tradition, without a written record whereby to test it, inevitably becomes corrupt. They are the absolute standard of a pure revelation, "according to which all doctrines and all teachers are to be judged." The fruits of Christian experience are not to be ignored by the student of theological science; but they are not coordinated with Holy Scripture, neither do they supplement Scripture. They are valuable, only as, when we recur to Holy Scripture, we find that they are the development of the truths therein set forth. The definitions of the Church are not to be lightly esteemed, nor is the testimony of Christian scholars of all ages to be passed by; but heartily as we admire, and profoundly as we study them, unless they can show that their divergence from the Scriptural record, is only in applying its truths to other spheres and other relations, they are to be absolutely discarded.

As long as the Apostles lived, endowed as witnesses of the teaching of the Lord, with a special divine gift which raised them above the possibility of error, this was of itself a sufficient standard. But when with their death, the Church was destitute of infallible teachers, the need of a record as the test of the pure apostolic teaching was manifest. Even the most ordinary matters of life, concerning which the witnesses have no motive for deception, are soon misrepresented, as the account passes by oral communication from person to person. The interest of the various persons who hear the report differs with respect to the details, according to the temperament, occupation, experience and education of each one. Every detail may be preserved, but the narrative will convey an entirely different impression, according to the varied emphasis of details, where a less important circumstance is assigned the chief place, and the most important sinks into relative obscurity. Thus the proportion of events is distorted. But the difficulty of accurate transmission increases, as the facts pass from the sphere of the natural to that of the super natural. What we understand we can transmit more faithfully than that which baffles our efforts to comprehend. The mysteries of faith would soon be distorted, were they not fixed in a written record. Still greater, however, is the difficulty where what is handed down reproves and condemns those by whom it is to be reported; where the dignity of humanity, concerning which men boast so loudly, is shown to be a fraud; where human wisdom is declared to be folly, and human glory dishonor; where, on every page, the very best man must read a reproof of sin and, but for the interposition of redemption, the certain wrath of God. We all know how natural it is to try to persuade ourselves that a charge against us is less serious than the reality. It is an easy matter to pass over specifications of guilt, and to suppress or misstate doctrines that to a perverted reason seem unimportant or absurd. The same principle that requires us to learn the standpoint of the historian, in order that we may estimate the correctness and proportioning of his facts, clearly declares that the statements of tradition are always influenced by the medium through which they come to us. In all important business transactions, mere oral statements are nothing. Everything is in uncertainty, until what is in mind is "put into black and white" in a writ ten document. An entertainment which is said to have originated with the late Prof. Whewell, of Cambridge, gives an excellent illustration. Write a brief narrative, and read it to the first of a circle of friends. Let him repeat it to his neighbor, and so on, until the last of the circle commits it to writing; and then let the two records be compared. But if, instead of continuous repetition, a year, or even a day should intervene between each repetition, and there should be some items included in the story discreditable to those who repeat it, it would soon assume a form that could scarcely be recognized. Scripture, therefore, is not to be brought to tradition, as the standard according to which it is to be tested, but tradition is constantly to be tested by Scripture. The final appeal is to the written record.

A record of revelation was necessary, also, in view of the large number of persons who were to be reached, and the closer and more frequent contact with revealed truth which was thus to be established. The oral tradition, even if preserved in its purity, could not always be recalled; most of it would be absent when most wanted. A sermon unwritten, however excellent, may soon be almost entirely forgotten even by the preacher, while the manuscript of former years recalls what otherwise is lost. If oral tradition were the test, then were any truth assailed by errorists, believers would be powerless, when they could not immediately recall the words of God upon which it rests; but with revelation committed to writing, the volume is always by them in which they can search and read for themselves what God has declared.

The authority of Holy Scripture is determined by inspiration. Revelation and inspiration are sometimes confounded. The former is the making known of that which hitherto had been unknown; the latter is the divine influence whereby men are enabled to produce an infallible declaration of what has been revealed. Inspiration with respect to the Holy Scriptures, is that divine act whereby chosen men were enabled to write an infallible record of revelation. So penetrating and thorough was this Divine influence, that the record is properly said to be the Word of God. The individuality of the writer is not destroyed. His peculiarities of style and thought are preserved, and this is done by no accommodation of the Holy Spirit to his phrases and idioms. The Gospel of St. Matthew is truly, and not simply seemingly, what it claims to be, the Gospel according to St. Matthew, i.e., the Gospel from the standpoint of the human personality of St. Matthew, with that personality impelled by the Spirit of God and guarded from all theological error. The grammar and rhetoric, like the chirography and orthography of the original text, are Matthew's. The entire human side of the Gospel comes from the writer. But, at the same time, every word is just as truly a word of the Holy Spirit. The Holy Spirit impelled the author to write, suggested the thoughts, and so controlled their expression, that it became an infallible record of revelation in all those matters for which God has given us a revelation. We claim for the Holy Scriptures absolute inerrancy with respect to all theological truth; we reject any suggestion or suspicion of deception, or error in the strict sense of the term, even on those subjects which only form the frame work, but not the contents of the record of revelation. It is true that the sun rises and sets, even though astronomy may in its way establish the contrary; for this deceives no reader, and conveys an entirely correct impression. No witness would be charged with perjury, if he swore that, at sunrise, he was witness of an important deed. Only a pedant would suggest that he spoke inaccurately. A Newton or a Kepler would always speak in the same way, except when he would enter upon the scientific explanation of the phenomenon of the rising and the setting sun. Writers were not inspired so as to speak with scientific precision when they employed their human knowledge of geographical or chronological details, in unfolding to unlettered men the revealed truth with which the entire range of human facts was connected. As in the person of Christ, the divine and the human were united, and, by this union, the limitation of the human element was not at once removed. The human element in Scripture reminds us of the human nature of Christ during the State of Humiliation. As Christ, in His humanity, refrained from the full use of the attributes communicated through its union with the divine nature, and thus shared in all the sinless weaknesses of humanity; so the Holy Spirit, in making the sacred writers infallible recorders of the hitherto unknown will of God towards men, in no way inspired them to be teachers of astronomy, or geology, or physics. These spheres do not belong to revelation. It is enough for us to know that, on these subjects, they had in the fullest extent the ordinary assistance granted believers even now, when, praying for the Spirit's guidance, they use earthly things in the service of the truth as it is in Jesus. No number of contradictions that could be gathered within this sphere, would in the least degree shake our confidence in the absolute authority of Holy Scripture as the in fallible test of theological truth, an inerrant guide in all matters of faith and practice. If it be fallible, then the very end for which a record of revelation has been provided, is defeated.

Holy Scripture carries with it its own evidence of its divine source and authority. While the historical evidence of its claims is to be gratefully cherished, and affords the proof of highest probability, Holy Scripture speaks with absolute certainty to those to whom it portrays the deepest secrets of their hearts, and whose felt wants it completely supplies. The inner testimony of the Spirit is the strongest and most convincing of all arguments. The fact that this is always at hand and universally applicable, raises it above all arguments that depend upon the researches of the learned. Here is an argument that the humblest and most unlettered apprehend with no less force than the profoundest scholars. This argument demands that whatever Holy Scripture claims for itself must be conceded; for if its testimony concerning itself be invalidated, how can it be trusted when it speaks of other things?

Holy Scripture is not only an infallible, but it is also a complete record of God's revelation. As revelation has had its degrees, the record of revelation has corresponded to them. God from the beginning disclosed to men all that was needful, at each particular stage of the world's history, for their salvation. Whatever fuller knowledge is unfolded, as we pass from one period to another, came by a fuller revelation, which was embodied in a fuller record. We need not seek beyond Scripture for any supplementary knowledge. Whatever is valuable in the experience of the Church is only a development, but not a supplement of the truth contained in Scripture.

Holy Scripture is also a sufficiently clear revelation. On every page we read mysteries whose depths the knowledge of an archangel cannot fathom. We constantly encounter difficulties which defy our reason, but must be cheerfully acquiesced in by our faith. Were its mysteries always intelligible, it would carry within it the proof of its own untrustworthiness. The revelation of an infinite God cannot be comprehended by finite man. Faith must rest upon that which we cannot see or understand. Hence the rule: "The things of Scripture are obscure; the words of Scripture are clear." The statement of the mysteries of religion is most clear, completely as the mysteries themselves transcend our thought. The fact revealed we can apprehend, unable as we are to comprehend the mode in which the fact exists, or the relations which it bears. Scripture is its own interpreter. Scripture as the revelation of a God of truth must be self-consistent. Every passage of Scripture must be read in the light of the context, and of other passages of Scripture bearing on the same subject. Scripture has but one sense, and is to be received literally, except where it demands for itself a figurative interpretation. When controversies arise, the original languages alone afford the accurate decision of the meaning; since it is only the Scriptures, as written in the original languages that are inspired. Even the best translation is only a human explanation or interpretation of the inspired words, however well the inspired thought may be conveyed in other language. But above all, the Scriptures require the enlightening influences of the Holy Spirit. While "the natural man receives not the things of the Spirit of God; for they are foolishness unto him: neither can he know them, because they are spiritually discerned," "he that is spiritual judges all things" (1 Cor. 2:14-15). If the clear light that shines from the Scriptures fails to enlighten sufficiently men's minds, it is because an obstruction is placed before the influences of the Spirit, as they seek to enter man and communicate the saving knowledge of the Gospel. This is the reason why ignorant men and women are sometimes more learned in the Scriptures, and more trustworthy interpreters than, in many respects, well-furnished theologians, Matt. 11:25. The Holy Spirit alone gives the key to unlock its treasures. A new sense must be created by His presence—a spiritual sense—or what is taught in Scripture will be misunderstood and misinterpreted, or be wrongly applied, or be apprehended and taught in the wrong order and in improper proportions. Important as this influence is, it is never separated from the

Scriptures; for wherever the Holy Scriptures are read or heard, there is the Holy Spirit present to at once interpret whatever strikes the eye or ear.

CHAPTER III
GOD

NEXT to the fact of our own existence, there is no truth so deeply fixed in our minds, or so constantly present to our thoughts, as that of the existence of God. No argument is required to establish it. It comes to man without and before his ability to appreciate any chain of reasoning whereby an attempt is made to demonstrate its certainty. It is a universal truth. Wherever there are men, there the existence of God and man's accountability to God are recognized. Among the most degraded men the fact may be greatly obscured, or be so thoroughly perverted, that sometimes it cannot be readily recognized, but it is still there. A more thorough investigation and closer examination of facts will always disclose it. Men have to reason themselves away from the thought of God, in order to reach the conclusion that this universal testimony of man's consciousness is a delusion.

No one, therefore, has been persuaded to believe that there is a God from the arguments adduced in Natural

Theology; just, as no one has been reasoned into the belief of his own existence by any philosophical demonstrations. As we need no demonstration of the existence of an external world, so we need no demonstration of the existence of God. A careful consideration, however, of the arguments ordinarily adduced for the existence of God, shows that instead of being proofs, they are rather the results of the effort of the human mind to analyze the ever-present idea of God. They do not so much establish the fact of God's existence, as they teach some of His attributes. Thus, the so-called cosmological argument, or that from effect to cause, affirms His power as operative in Creation and Providence. The teleological argument, or argument from design, affirms His wisdom and love. The ontological argument affirms His infinity. The moral argument affirms His holiness and justice.

We are not persuaded of God's existence by the assumption that the thought of God is innate. The history of the process by which this thought first came to us, is an interesting subject of investigation; but the fact that we have ever before us the evidences of His presence is the most important. We are not satisfied with looking back to a revelation which God once made, and tracing its tradition. Nearer and clearer and far more overwhelming than any argument drawn from innate ideas or historical evidences, is the one which meets man face to face every day and hour of his life. Everywhere we see the traces of an unseen Hand; everywhere we hear the voice of an unseen Speaker. Wherever we go, we are limited by His power and controlled by His wisdom. He breathes in every breath that we draw, acts in every act we put forth, and lives in all our lives. We know His existence and presence just as certainly as we do that of our very nearest friend. The mother is no more conscious of the life of her child, than we are of that of God. We may be isolated from all human beings, and yet we can never be alone; for when we seem most alone, we are alone with God. As I look through my window, I see a majestic tree. Do I need, in order to be sure of its existence, to analyze my conception of the tree, and to trace the process by which it is presented to my consciousness, and to gather a large store of arguments to be accurately examined by metaphysicians? There it stands, and I am not affected in my knowledge of its existence by all my reasoning. The convincing argument is that of the restored blind man in John 9:25: "One thing I know, that, whereas I was blind, now I see." So we know that there is a God, because He is inseparable from our thought and experience.

No argument for the existence of God is needed, where Holy Scripture is accepted as an authorized record of His revelation; since this is presupposed on every page. These arguments can enter into consideration in Theology, only as, with the existence of God acknowledged, the various elements contained in our conception of God are analyzed and traced to their first sources. But, as the truth contained in Holy Scripture, is after all only an external matter to the unregenerate man; so the conception of God is weak and faint in the unregenerate, when compared to that which is attained by the regenerate man, who in his daily experience not only has the fact of God's existence brought vividly to mind, but who constantly experiences more and more what God is. The unregenerate man knows that God is; the regenerate man has begun to know what God is. This knowledge continually grows, but never reaches perfection. Even in the world of bliss it passes knowledge.

The first element that is contained in our conception of God is that of personality. God is a person. Religion is a communion between two persons, viz.: between man and God. If God were a mere idea or a force, there could be no communion; or, if man and God were one, there could be no communion, and, therefore, no religion. Religion is a relation of person to person, viz.: of me here, to God both here and in Heaven. The communion between man and God is grounded upon the fact that both are personalities. All that is involved in the conception of personality, individuality, identity, self-consciousness, self-determination, is ascribed to God. An idea cannot think, an energy cannot act with reflection towards a self-determined end, and from self-determined motives; nor is either idea or energy self-conscious.

The second element in our conception of God is that of infinity. God is an infinite personality. His being transcends our highest thought. Sure as we are that we know Him, we are just as sure that our knowledge is limited, and that, with all possible expansion, it will never exhaust its subject. Man cannot comprehend God, because the finite cannot contain the infinite. The mysteries of God's being that defy all the efforts of our intellects to grasp, only confirm the truth of God's revelation; for a revelation that has no difficulties, cannot be the revelation of an infinite God. It is for communion with the Infinite that we yearn, and with nothing less will the heart be satisfied. We know God then, not as He is in Himself, but in so far as He has revealed Himself. But while our knowledge is thus limited, it is, as far as it goes, none the less real. Nor does the fact that this knowledge is finite, render it indefinite. It is the surest form of knowledge, because it is the self-revelation of the Being upon whom all else depends.

The third element is that of the nearness of God to all His creatures. His infinity does not render Him distant, but brings Him near to us. He is not a God afar off, enthroned above the highest star, but He pervades all time and all space with His presence, everywhere present and everywhere operative, Acts 17:27-28.

The various forms of skepticism arise from the appropriation of one or more elements of truth, and emphasizing it to the exclusion of the rest. Polytheism emphasizes the necessity of the personality of God, but defeats its end by ignoring His infinity. The multiplication of its deities is a self-contradiction. Pantheism emphasizes the infinity and constant and omnipresent activity of God, but ignores His personality, and thus is involved in another contradiction. Deism accepts His personality and infinity, but denies His constant and omnipresent activity, thus rendering communion with God, and God's revelation of Himself impossible. Agnosticism claims that because no complete revelation has been made, no partial revelation can be given; and that because we cannot know God as He is in Himself, we cannot know Him at all, or even know that He exists. It claims to know to a certainty that nothing can be known to a certainty, and thus commits intellectual suicide.

The general conception of God expressed by the combination of these elements, is made still more explicit by the enumeration of the Divine Attributes. The attributes of God are not mere human conceptions of what God is; for they have existence apart from and independently of our conception of them. For this reason, the definition of these attributes, as "inadequate conceptions of the Divine essence," once current in the schools, may be misleading. It is better to define them as the distinguishing characteristics of the Divine essence, or as the Divine essence revealing itself in various forms and relations. When the knowledge of these attributes enters the human mind, we can speak of the impressions made upon man as "inadequate conceptions," and, in this sense, may define them also as "the different relations in which the idea of God is present to the consciousness of the godly man." The attributes cannot be separated from the nature; they are the nature directed or determined in different ways and relations. As God cannot be comprehended, He reveals Himself to finite man by leading man to various standpoints from which the simple and indivisible nature of God may be regarded. While God's nature is not the sum of His attributes, our knowledge of His nature is the sum of our knowledge of His attributes.

But this does not imply that the distinction between the attributes exists only in the human mind, or in the Divine revelation as it accommodates itself to the human mind. The distinction is a real one, since the relations which they express are different. God's knowledge cannot (e.g.) be identified with His will; for the knowledge includes some things that the will excludes. Sin is an object of God's knowledge, but not of God's will.

All God's attributes are essential. In God there is no accident, that is, nothing that can be removed. Nothing can be added to His essence, and nothing can be subtracted from it. He cannot be increased or diminished. If the same attributes appear in angels or in men, they are accidental to them; while in God, they are essential.

Contrasting the conception of God, derived from Holy Scripture, with that of His creatures, as seen in the natural world, we must regard every excellence of the creature as existing in God in the highest perfection; we must regard every defect of the creature, as removed from God, and God as the source of all creatures and their excellences. The attributes may be classified according to the various arguments usually adduced to prove the divine existence. The most usual classification, however, has been that of immanent and transient, sometimes known as negative and positive attributes. The former have reference to God as He exists in Himself; the latter to God in His relations to creatures. Thus Eternity is an immanent attribute, and Goodness a transient attribute. These attributes are specifically enumerated in Holy Scripture. In considering them, it will sometimes be found that what are presented as two separate attributes, are only one fundamental attribute, considered in various relations. Thus Eternity and Immensity are Infinity; Eternity being Infinity in time, and Immensity being Infinity in space. Omnipotence, Omniscience and Omnipresence are only the same Infinity in other relations. Omnipotence in no way requires that everything is attributable to God, but only that what is a perfection be ascribed Him. To say that God could sin, would be to deny His Holiness; that He could lie, would deny His Truth; that He could cease to exist, would deny His Eternity. When, then, it is affirmed that it is impossible for God to die, we only affirm His Eternity and Immutability. We ascribe to God everything that does not imply a contradiction in His nature. So His Immensity does not deny His power of self-limitation. He was united with the humanity of Christ in a different way from that in which He subsists in other creatures; and He dwells in the godly in a different way from in the ungodly. He is above all limitations, except those which He Himself determines. His

Omnipresence is not by any expansion—all God is everywhere. As the soul, a finite, simple substance, is everywhere present in the body, so God, an infinite, simple Substance is everywhere present in the universe.

When emphasis is laid upon the free will of God it is distinguished from His natural will. The natural will is that which is determined by God's attributes; so that, were God to will anything contrary to His natural will, a contradiction would be involved. The natural is, therefore, a necessary will of God; it is the inevitable expression of His nature. But the free will is where God wills what He might have willed otherwise, as when He devised the plan of redemption, and willed to call Paul to the Apostolate.

The doctrine of the Trinity is deduced by a collection of three classes of passages of Holy Scripture, viz.: those which teach most clearly the divine unity; those which teach a plurality in God, and those which teach that there is a real, and not simply a formal or modal distinction indicated by the plurality. The entire teaching of Holy Scripture from beginning to end emphasizes the doctrine of the unity of God. There is one God, and besides Him none other. No less clearly, however, is it manifest that the name, the attributes, the works and the worship of God belong to the Father, the Son, and the Holy Ghost. Repeatedly, also, are they contrasted and distinguished from each other. They cannot be one person subsisting under three diverse forms, or appearing under three diverse manifestations. Nor can the Holy Ghost, with His personal names, personal works and personal worship, be simply a power or energy of God. There are, therefore, three persons in the one God.

> There is one person of the Father, another of the
> Son, and another of the Holy Ghost. The Father is
> God, and the Son is God, and the Holy Ghost is
> God. So there is one Father—not three Fathers; one
> Son—not three Sons; one Holy Ghost—not three
> Holy Ghosts. (Athanasian Creed)

This is what is meant by the expression, "three persons in one essence." The Church wrestles hard with the inadequate terms of human speech to describe this mystery. It can only be approximately, it cannot be adequately stated in any language. "The finite cannot comprehend the Infinite." None of the terms used for this purpose convey the precise meaning, that is conveyed when they are used in common speech. Father and Son and Holy Ghost are not distinct persons, in the same way that we note the distinct personality of Peter, James and John. The term "person" simply indicates as the Augsburg Confession declares: "not a part or quality in another, but that which subsists of itself."

There is no conflict between the doctrine of the personality of God, and the doctrine of the three personalities in the one God. The term "person" is used in the two cases for the purpose of emphasizing the true conception of God, as over against two different classes of errors. When the one God is called "one person," it is in antagonism to modern Pantheism, which regards Him as an unconscious and necessary force working in the world. When the one God is called "three persons," it is in opposition to ancient Sabellianism and Arianism. The seeming conflict is harmonized in the definition that God is "three persons in one absolute personality."

While "in this Trinity none is before or after other; none is greater or less than another," yet as the persons are distinct, there is an order in their revelation to men, and in their relation to one another to which this revelation corresponds. They have their distinctive characteristics and works. Of these, some are internal, and others external. To the former belong the eternal generation of the Son by the Father, the sending forth of the Holy Ghost by the Father and the Son, and the procession of the Holy Ghost from both Father and Son. Here again human language fails to do more than simply to suggest what is involved. It must constantly be borne in mind that the terms employed stand for no more than the one aspect of the truth which they are intended to designate, and must not be extended beyond that which can be manifestly justified by Scriptural statements. "Father, Son and Holy Ghost are one and the same divine essence, regarded as begetting, begotten and proceeding." The relation of father to son among men is only the incomplete reflection of Father to Son in the Trinity. If it be objected that this relation gives the Father a priority of existence, the illustration of the ancient divines is at hand, that the sun is no older than its rays.

While no passage of Holy Scripture expressly declares that the Holy Ghost proceeds from the Son as well as from the Father, and the only passage on the procession, John 15:26, refers it to the Father, without mention of the Son, nevertheless, the doctrine of the double procession rests upon firm arguments. The silence concerning the Son does not exclude Him. In John 14:26, the temporal sending, which we know from 15:26 to refer to both Father and Son, is referred to the Father alone. The sending of the Holy Ghost from both Father and Son, John 15:26; 16:7, is a most suggestive analogy. He is also called the Spirit of the Son, Romans 8:9; Galatians 4:6. When the equality of the Son with the Father is proved from other passages, the double procession necessarily follows; since otherwise the subordination of the Son to the Father is implied.

Analogies prove nothing, and furnish more points of difference than of resemblance; but they serve to illustrate. Such are the root, the plant, the flower and fruit; the spring, the brook, the river; the sun, with its shape, its light and heat, or the illuminating, calorific and chemical qualities of the sun's rays; the three-fold dimensions of space; the three-fold division of time; the three chords in music combined into one tone; the three parts of a proposition (subject, predicate and copula); the tripartite nature of man (body, soul and spirit); the three-fold faculties of the human mind (intellect, sensibilities, will). A modern amplification of an illustration of Augustine deduces the doctrine of the Trinity from the definition of God as love. For if God is love, this means one who loves, and one who is loved, and "a common object in whom their mutual love is triunified," viz.: Father, Son and Holy Ghost. "God conceived of as only I, as a mere subject, would be absolute egotism, and thus the very reverse of love."

Besides the internal characteristics of the persons of the Trinity, there are also those which are external. But here a different relation meets us. The internal characteristics are not common. Only the Father begat; only the Son is begotten. In the external characteristics (*opera ad extra*), all the persons participate and are alike active. The distinction does not belong to the works themselves, but to the prominence with which each person is revealed as participating in a work. Thus the Father is most prominent in Creation, the Son in

Redemption, and the Holy Ghost in Sanctification, but in no way exclusively or subordinately. In each work the Father acts through the Son in the Holy Ghost. The three persons being one God, are one Creator, one Redeemer, one Sanctifier.

CHAPTER IV
GOD AS CREATOR: ANGELS

THE world had a beginning. The act by which God gave it a beginning was Creation. It was not a mere reforming and reshaping of pre-existing material, but that, properly, by which what had previously no existence whatever was brought into existence. This is known as Immediate Creation. The doctrine of a Mediate Creation, or reshaping of what had preexisted, is not inconsistent with that of Immediate Creation, but must not be regarded as Creation in the proper sense.

Once God was alone in the Universe. Neither spirit or matter was present except in His eternal thought. If Creation can be said to be eternal, it is only as the purpose of Creation was ever before Him.

Creation came from God's free will, not from His natural will; since Creation was not a necessity of His nature. The world is, therefore, not an emanation from God's substance, which would be inconsistent with His personality and simplicity. It is not a part of God, or God, but a distinct object, called forth from absolute nothingness by His command. The Omnipotence of God thus comes first to view in Creation, as we confess in the First Article of the Apostle's Creed.

God called other beings into existence, in order to communicate to them His own goodness and happiness. In communicating these gifts, He manifests His glory in the highest degree. The glory of His power and wisdom is subordinate to the glory of His self-communicating goodness. The attributes of His nature are employed in the service of His beneficent will.

The anthropocentric doctrine of Creation, is clearly taught in Holy Scripture, Ps. 8:6; 115:16. God created all things for the sake of man; and man He created for Himself. For while the Order of Creation made man lower than the angels, the ultimate goal of Redemption was in view, by which man was to be exalted above the angels through a salvation, in the application of which angels were to be man's servants. All things were created that man might eternally recognize and enjoy God's goodness, and eternally worship and adore Him.

The agent of Creation was the personal Word. All things were made by Him, who was made flesh and dwelt among us, John 1:3, 14. This belongs to His office as the Revealer of the counsels of the Godhead, Creation being the first act of Revelation.

Creation and Providence are distinguished formally, but not in reality. Creation may be regarded as the beginning of that activity which is continued in Providence, or Providence in the widest sense, may be made to include Creation. In its usual meaning, it is restricted to that series of acts by which God sustains the creatures that He has called into being, directs them to the end for which He has created them, and overrules even their perversity and resistance of His will to the highest good of men and the glory of His name.

We cannot treat the doctrine of Providence except from the standpoint of Redemption. All our conceptions of it are connected with the overruling and directing agency of God in a world of sin, for the purpose of carrying out to completion His redemptive work. While, therefore, the doctrine of Providence logically precedes the consideration of Redemption, yet it comprises so many particulars belonging properly to the latter sphere, that we defer it until then.

In like manner, the doctrine of angels includes some details that are presupposed in the treatment of sin and redemption, and others which follow it. The knowledge afforded on this subject is small. It enters into the experience of no Christian of today. It depends entirely upon the testimony of Scripture passages which introduce us to them, only so far as they are connected with man's relation to sin and redemption. They come only occasionally to notice at great epochs in the progress of the Kingdom of God.

They are not the glorified spirits of the departed, as popular representations sometimes say. The blessed dead are like the angels, Matt. 22:30, but are not angels. Angels are like men in being created and finite spiritual beings; they differ from men by being complete spirits. Man needs a body for the completion of his being. Angels belong to a higher order of things than does man. They are independent of the limitations and conditions of the world of sense. Hence the attributes of invisibility, immateriality, indivisibility, incorruptibility, are ascribed to them. As finite, their presence cannot be the Omnipresence of God (repletive); but as spirits, their presence cannot be subject to the laws of space. It is the presence of simple spirits (definitive), a presence which cannot be resolved into parts, as the different parts of a body have different relations to parts of space. This is sometimes called an illocal presence, not because it is not presence at a place, but because its modes are not subject to the laws of space. Like the spiritual part of man's being, they are immortal, although created with a liability to spiritual death. Hence their immutability, when contrasted with that of God, is only relative. When they become visible, it is through bodies which they have temporarily assumed.

All their relation to men is only that of one finite cause to another. Their activity cannot absolutely destroy the powers of nature or man's free will. They make use of the means pertaining to the spheres within which they work, either by assuming human forms or employing the forces of Nature, Ps. 114:4; Heb. 1:7. Their connection with the world in which we live does not appear to be a constant or habitual one; it has all the rarity of a miracle, and marks certain great epochs or most important events in the development of God's purposes. The exception in the case of Satan belongs to the perversion of his original creation.

All our knowledge of angels is subordinate to the knowledge we have of man. Their existence, nature and works, their original condition, the test to which they were subjected, and the two classes into which they were subsequently divided, have been revealed, in order that we may understand the better man's own relations and destiny and history.

CHAPTER V
GOD AS CREATOR: MAN

MAN came into existence by a special creative act of God. Even though theistic evolutionists were able to establish their claims—for which they have given no sufficient evidence—that man's body has come from the dust of the ground through a process of gradual development from the lower animals, this by no means explains man's higher life, which alone makes man man. The body without the spirit, "breathed into his nostrils" by God, Gen. 2:7, is not man. The immaterial principle in human nature is in Holy Scripture sometimes called soul, and sometimes spirit. Man is sometimes said to be composed of soul and body, and, at other times, of spirit and body. In other passages, soul and spirit are contrasted with each other. The distinction is not between two different things, or parts, but the reference is to the same immaterial thing, as viewed on its earthward and on its heavenward side, or between the lower and the higher qualities of man's spiritual nature. They are not separate parts of man's being, but are clearly distinguished; the soul referring to the subject of life, and the spirit to that subject as endowed with a peculiar divinely-communicated life.

The image of God, in which man was created, was not properly-speaking man's personality. This was only the ground or basis of the image. Like God, man has self-consciousness, and, within certain limitations, man has also freedom. Philosophically speaking, these may be described as factors of the image. But they do not constitute or belong to the image which Holy Scripture describes as man's original endowment, and as lost by the Fall. This was rather "the reflection of the infinite, divine fullness of attributes in the finite spirit of man," so that what belongs to God as an infinite, was found in man as a finite being. What belonged to God absolutely belonged to man relatively. Hence man was not the image of God, as the Son is said to be in Heb. 1:3; Col. 1:15, but he was created in the image, after the likeness of God, Gen. 1:26. The Son of God was, therefore, the model according to which man was created. The attributes of God which were particularly prominent in man, and whose importance can be estimated by their loss, are those of knowledge, righteousness and holiness, Col. 3:10; Eph. 4:24.

Hence this image was not man's nature, but a determination of this nature, or mode in which the nature existed. Nor, on the other hand, was it something added to the nature; for the image was contemporaneous with the origin of man's nature. The possibility of its loss without the destruction of the nature, indicated simply a possibility of a change of condition.

Man was created to be completely happy and completely holy. As the image of God, he was to reflect in a finite creature, the happiness and holiness of the infinite

Creator. Without this image, there can be happiness as little as there can be holiness. Where the image has been lost, the sole hope of happiness lies in the restoration of the image.

Holy and happy as man was when created, there were within him possibilities for the infinite development of all that the divine image included. The reflection of the Infinite within the finite, implied that the finite should ever approach more nearly to the perfection of the Infinite. The image of God in Adam was only the feeblest germ of what was to proceed from it. The acorn may be as perfect, in its sphere, as the oak; but this does not imply that the one is not intended to grow into the other. The perfection of humanity is dependent upon the unfolding of its capacities, as the perfection of the seed requires that it should germinate and yield fruit.

Connected with this possibility of infinite development, was also the possibility of a fall and the loss of the image. The highest perfection was in fact to be attained by a struggle with a deterrent force. The capacity for higher holiness was to be gained by the knowledge of that with which it is directly contrasted. Negative holiness was to be succeeded by a positive and aggressive holiness, which was to prove itself in contact with evil. The highest happiness was to emerge from an experience with the misery which is its opposite. God's glory itself was to be most brilliantly displayed upon the background of sin and guilt.

CHAPTER VI
SIN

THROUGH this experience of humanity, the angels had already passed. The possibility of a fall by the abuse of their free wills was the condition by which the perfection of the angelic nature was attained. In the contact and conflict with evil, all angelic attributes on the part of those who bore the test, advanced to a higher stage and a wider range. It was their native endowment to have the capacity to reach a perfection which would be beyond the power of any abuse of their free wills. Absolute moral immutability is an attribute of God alone. The moral immutability of men and angels is relative and derived. That some fell and others did not, was due to no difference in the grace which God bestowed. No angel was created, no man was created or born with such support from God, that he could not be otherwise than holy, or do otherwise than right. To claim that for man, is to claim for man an attribute of God. The mystery of the permission of a fall, ultimately must resolve itself into the question why man was not invested with other divine attributes, or must lead to such un answerable questions concerning man's original condition when contrasted with his future destiny, as, e. g., why the body of Adam was not endowed with the spiritual properties which are to belong to the resurrection body. It is enough to learn from His declared will what was God's purpose, and not to inquire concerning the reasons that God has not revealed.

We cannot trace the origin of evil beyond the fact that a being higher than man, created in holiness, voluntarily turned from God and became God's enemy. It is needless to speculate as to what was the particular sin from temptation to which Satan fell, or as to whether since the temptation was self-originated, the fall had not already occurred with the suggestion of the sin. Nothing but labyrinths open from such questions.

The attempts in modern times to discredit the Biblical doctrine of a personal devil are readily answered. The absence of a personal tempter, who first fell himself, and then led others into ruin, implies greater difficulties than can be alleged against his presence. When it is urged that there could be no motive for a fall, it is answered that, whatever may have been the motive, the fall consisted in the turning of his free will towards the object presented, and away from God. "That the devil has fallen from pride, means only that, by an act of his free will, he perverted his original humility into diabolical pride." The presence of the alternative of good or evil as a possibility, and the consciousness of that alternative on his part did not imply a defect of his nature. It only furnished what was intended to advance the higher development of his angelic perfection. It became evil by the wrong determination of his free will towards it.

If it be objected that Satan's persistence in sin is inconsistent with the remarkable prudence and knowledge that is ascribed to him, even since the fall, the answer is at hand, that illustrations of such inconsistency can be readily furnished in the experience of men. Sin is proverbially short sighted. Whatever cunning may attend it, is so biased by impulse that it defeats itself. The most exquisite acuteness and quickness are often combined with the most defective judgment. Mere knowledge is no barrier to a fall.

If the possibility of any organized empire of evil under Satan as leader be denied because of the antagonism of the demons to one another, an effectual answer is supplied by conspiracies of wicked men. Bands of robbers have their chiefs and their laws. Schemes of fraud and violence are not infrequently thoroughly organized.

The personality of Satan is not, therefore, a non-fundamental doctrine. With it stand or fall the Biblical doctrines of sin and redemption. *Nullus diabolus, nullus redemptor.*

The fact that it was a pure spirit, with whom sin originated, answers the suggestion more frequently underlying certain conceptions of sin, than formally expressed, that sin is more or less closely connected with that which is material, or corporeal.

Sin was the act of a free spirit turning from God. Sin has been diffused by the continued agency of a spirit upon other spirits. Incidentally or accidently, matter is used only as the organ or instrument of the sin of the spirit.

The fall of Satan was followed by the fall of other holy spirits. While to Satan the temptation came from within, to them the temptation came from without, John 8:44. With the loss of holiness, they suffered also an impairment of all the qualities which belonged to their nature. Great as is their power, Eph. 6: 12, it is limited to such a degree that, by God's grace, feeble men and women overcome it. Their punishment has already begun. Much as they rage against God, and direct their efforts against His kingdom, they are, nevertheless, in chains, 2 Pet. 2:4; Jude, ver. 6, and anticipate the coming wrath of God on the Day of Judgment, Matt. 8:29.

As sin preceded man's sin, and as man's sin was simply the result of a contagion of sin which he could have repelled and prevented from finding lodgment within him, a consideration of the nature of sin itself very appropriately comes before the account of man's fall.

Sin is to be otherwise than God means us to be, and to do otherwise than God means us to do. It presupposes freedom. For whatever be God's will with respect to angels and men, He does not will that, against their own will, they shall comply with His will. The holiness of the creature consists alone in the harmonizing of his will with that of God. Sin has its root and nature in the determination of the freewill away from God. If angels or men ultimately attain a stage of perfection, in which they are removed from the possibility of doing otherwise, or being otherwise than God desires, such impeccability is not an original endowment, but is the fruit and reward of effort and struggle. The holiness in which men and angels were created was an undeveloped holiness, viz., a potential, but not an absolute impeccability.

Nevertheless, God had for humanity a goal that He wished it to attain, and which he placed within its power. His permission did not imply indifference as to the result. There was but one choice which could meet His approval. Wherever a choice different from this is found, there is sin.

The choice which would meet God's approval He has defined in His Law. Sin is the want of conformity with God's Law. The Law is the declaration of the immutable will of God concerning what He would have us be, do or omit to do. Hence, sin can be just as properly described as the want of conformity with God's will, as the want of conformity with God's Law, since the Law is only the will as proclaimed and enjoined.

As also the Law demands of us as truly what we must be, as what we must do, a temper, a disposition, a habit of mind and thought, as well as acts of obedience, sin is as truly a state, as it is an act, the being otherwise than God wishes us to be, as well as the doing otherwise than God wishes us to do. When God's Law requires us to love God with all our hearts, the not loving God is as truly sin, as any act of transgression it were possible for us to commit.

The state of sin, however, was entered, on the part of angels and men, by a particular act of sin. The habit of obedience to God once broken, a state of sin followed, all whose acts were also sin.

The relation of men to one another differs from that of angels to one another. This results in a difference in the relation of the first sin of angels to that of the rest, from that of the first sin of men to that of other men. The angels were without organic union with one another. Each angel stood or fell by and for himself. The fall of no one carried others down with him. For the angels neither begat, nor were begotten. There could be no race sin. But all men have an organic relation with one another. The sum total of humanity was in the first pair. By their obedience, the race would have risen above the possibility of a fall. By their disobedience, the whole race fell with them into the state of sin. The ability to love and fear God was lost by the race. By the abuse of the free will of our first parents, the race became otherwise than God meant that it should be. The original righteousness and holiness were lost. Man could no longer be what God would have him, if he would; and he would not, if he could. Not only was the ability to serve God lost, but the will was directed against all that pleased God. Man not only ceased to love God, but he delighted in whatever displeased God. All of man's endowments and faculties were perverted and disordered. As the children inherited the diseases and sufferings of their parents, so also, they inherited their sin. The race sin incurred by Adam, became the common property of all his descendants. The personal sins resulting from Adam's first sin were not propagated, but the one sin, both in act and state, from which they came, descended from father to child.

Just as indissolubly connected as are holiness and happiness, are sin and misery. Righteousness and God's favor, guilt and God's wrath belong together. The union of God with man, was man's life, as first created; the division of God from man by man's apostasy and sin, was his death. For what the soul is to the body, that God is to the soul. Man had turned from God, and involuntarily lost God, and could not regain Him, until God would Himself re-enter into a communion of life and love with man.

CHAPTER VII
THE WAGES OF SIN

THE effects of sin were not realized at once. The first act was simply the beginning of an infinite series. From the state of sin, there was to come a process, that, if not interminable, was, at all events, not to be terminated. With sin, came death, designated from its three-fold stages, death spiritual, temporal and eternal.

Death spiritual occurred instantaneously with man's sin. A soul without God is already dead. It is absolutely incapable of disposing itself in any way in harmony with God's will. The freedom of the will in external things remains to an extent; but the freedom of the will in spiritual things is absolutely gone. The will of a sinful man is free to choose between two alternatives, or to accept or reject an offered object; but whatever alternative it chooses, and whether it accept or reject what is offered, it only sins. It is absolutely helpless in spiritual things, until God bestows upon it new powers by re-uniting man to Himself, and infusing within man a new life. Spiritual death, however, implies growth in moral corruption. The potencies of evil are more and more unfolded. The career downward continues with ever increasing force. A sinful race deteriorates, as time advances, and individuals are hardened in crime with their years. A most graphic picture of this is portrayed by St. Paul at the close of the first chapter of Romans. The process continues not simply by the natural development of evil, but especially by the active agency of Satan, to whose control the children of disobedience have been consigned. In this state of spiritual death, all descendants of Adam and Eve were born.

Temporal death is only another stage of the process. As men linger for years, dying inch by inch from a fatal wound, that is gradually sapping their strength, so the death of the body begins with the death of the soul. As the process of decomposition begins the moment the soul has left the body, so the moment man sinned, the body became the abode of diseases and pains, of which it had previously been incapable, "In the day that you eat thereof, you will surely die" (Gen. 2:17), had thus a literal fulfillment. The soul would undoubtedly have been at once removed from the body, if it had not been for the interposition of redemption. The future sacrifice on Calvary was prospectively interposed for the sins of the world, and, through this interposition, humanity continued to exist on earth, and to develop, with the prospect of recovery for every soul infected with the contagion, as it descends from parent to child.

The full penalty of sin is eternal death. The essence of eternal death is eternal sin and eternal guilt. Eternal death, is to be separated from God without any hope of reunion with Him. It is to feel the misery of sin, and to be conscious of the impossibility of redemption. It is to be brought face to face with guilt, without the intervention of that Divine mercy which delayed the complete execution of the sentence of the Fall. It has its stages and degrees. It begins with the separation of the soul from the body. In a world of conscious pain and misery, the soul awakens when it passes from this life. It is full of regrets for the lost opportunities and abused privileges of earth. It is in anguish over the remembrance of sins. It has not lost all its sympathies for those whom it has left behind, and before whom it clearly perceives the same judgment impending, beneath which it is suffering. Still more dreadful is the prospect which rises before it in the future. Poignant as is the sorrow, directly succeeding death, another crisis is approaching with the Day of Judgment. What man has suffered before in the soul alone, he must suffer then with increased severity in body and soul. Only then does he enter the place prepared for the devil and his angels, and meet the full penalty for the things done in his body. What occurs with the fallen angels, occurs also with man. Although cast down and delivered into chains of darkness, what is peculiarly the "time" of their torment awaits them.

There is not the least glimmer of hope of any cessation or alleviation of the punishment for those who suffer eternal death. It is a death which does not bring any absolute extinction or annihilation. When called "destruction," the process only whereby God's wrath descends eternally, is most forcibly described. The doctrine of "conditional immortality" has no warrant in God's Word. Shrink from the contemplation of the ceaseless, conscious miseries of those who eternally sin, as we may, the reality is not lessened. We can only pray God to be delivered from the penalties our sins have merited, and be diligent as instruments to bring God's grace and mercy to others. Neither can we find any warrant for the hope that there may be repentance after death, and that those who have persevered in sin to the last moment of life, may be reclaimed in the world to come. The state of both righteous and unrighteous will then be unalterably fixed.

PART II

The **PREPARATION** of REDEMPTION

CHAPTER VIII
THE GROUND AND GOAL, OF REDEMPTION

THE entire race has fallen. Every human being has lost his opportunity for being so confirmed in good by an act of his free will, as to be beyond the possibility of losing holiness and God's favor. The possibility has been followed by a fearful reality. Humanity has become a mass of corruption. Everywhere there is only sin and ruin. The only prospect of any change is as the ruin and corruption become still more intense, or still further unfold capacities of guilt and suffering. God has done His part to bring man to the highest holiness and happiness; but man has repelled God's effort. If there be no new interference on God's part, man will perish by his own fault. God can, in no way, be chargeable with man's death. It would have been only just, if the whole race had been eternally deserted to the consequences of its rejection of

God. Salvation could be asked for, not on the ground of justice, but solely of mercy. The smallest particle of mercy shown, could not be used, as the basis of any complaint why more mercy should not be shown. God would shown, could not be used, as the basis of any complaint why more mercy should not be shown. God would not be unjust, if His mercy would not be as comprehensive as His justice.

The fallen angels were justly left to the full consequences of their transgression. If man's lot had been the same, he would not have been wronged. Since man's lot is different, the fallen angels are not wronged. Injustice cannot be complained of, where there is the suffering only of that which is the just due of the sufferer. If, then, God had determined by some other means, to satisfy the demands of His justice for but one man who was condemned to eternal death, and to free him from the consequences of the Fall, there could have been no just complaint on the part of the numberless millions to whom such mercy would not have been shown. God is free to show mercy to whom He will show mercy; and the withholding of mercy is no act of injustice. If His mercy would comprehend ten or a hundred, or a thousand, or a million of elect, none passed by would be wronged. Nor would He be unjust, if all mankind except a million, or a thousand, or a hundred would be forgiven. The case is extreme, but nevertheless it is true,—if His mercy were such that a plan of Salvation would be provided for all the human race, except for me,—if I alone of all who have ever lived, or who are to live, would be passed by, where would be the injustice, as long as I am enduring no more than the just recompense of my sin? Because I may choose to forgive a debtor his debt, there is no obligation resting upon me to cancel the debts of all who owe me. Nor does my canceling the debts even of most of my debtors, bind me to extinguish those of all. A debtor can ask for favors, but he cannot demand them as rights. Not upon the grounds of abstract justice, but solely upon those of the revelation of His purpose must our determination of the extent of any plan of grace God may devise, depend.

For God has a plan of grace for fallen men. It is as eternal as God's knowledge of man's Fall. God created man, in order to redeem him. Redemption is no after-thought in God's mind, simply for the purpose of counteracting and thwarting what He either could or would not prevent. We may separate in our thoughts the Orders of Creation and Redemption, but they could not be separated in God's thought. The world was created, in order that, in Redemption, it might be the theatre for the display of God's love. However marred and defaced by sin, these blemishes are only to be made to contribute to a higher glory. All the pain and suffering that sin has brought, from the standpoint of Redemption, point to a closer union with, and a higher enjoyment of God. What is lost in Adam is far more than regained in Christ. Where sin abounded, grace is to super-abound. By the Order of Creation, man is made a little lower than the angels; by the Order of Redemption, he is raised above the angels. According to the mind and purpose of God, who sees the end from the beginning, and, who comprehends in one simple plan, what seem to us to be diverse or complex plans, man was created, in order, by the appropriation of Redemption, through a long continued conflict with sin, to attain among God's countless creatures and highest intelligences, the very next place to the throne of God Himself. Man was created, in order that God might assume man's nature, cover all the faults and defects of that nature, pay the penalty for all the sins and bear all the sorrows of that nature, that man's nature, thus redeemed, might rise from its humiliation and mortality, to share eternally the blessedness and glory of God's own nature.

CHAPTER IX
GOD'S ETERNAL PURPOSE

Redemption, on the one hand, is as comprehensive as the ruin wrought in human nature by sin; on the other, it is limited to only a portion of the human race. It is as comprehensive in its provisions as it is limited in its realization. As it was God's will that humanity should persevere in its concreated holiness, only so far as man's exercise of his free will towards the offered good and evil would not be interfered with, so it was God's purpose that all should enjoy redemption, provided the power of the decision of man's free will against the offered good be not destroyed. Grace has to do with persons, and their very personality implies, along with self-consciousness, self-determination. While man is helpless to deliver himself, or to prepare himself for divine grace, or even to respond to this grace as it approaches him, and thus his acceptance of God's grace comes from new powers which grace has brought, nevertheless, the freedom of the will is still preserved in man's ability to resist God's grace. All man's help must thus come from God; all his ruin comes from himself.

The provisions of Redemption, therefore, are ample for all. Not only do the Holy Scriptures declare that they are sufficient for all, but directly and explicitly that they have been made and are intended for all. Every human life that enters this world is that of a redeemed child of God. Every child is born, both a child of wrath and a child of grace. It is a child of wrath, since by inheritance its state is that of spiritual death. It is a child of grace, in so far as it has been comprised in the Scheme of Redemption and the love and mercy of God that devised the scheme, go forth in efforts for the application to it of this Redemption. It remains a child of wrath so far as the efforts of divine grace to aid it are defeated by the persevering resistance of its will. It becomes a child of grace, not only potentially, but in reality, when divine grace over comes the natural resistance of its will, and it submits to God; the state of regeneration succeeding that of spiritual death.

The results of this contact of divine grace with every human heart have been comprehended in the divine Omniscience from all eternity. God knows fully the end from the beginning. He has ever held in His memory and surveyed the secrets of all hearts. The so-called "instantaneous process" of photography records upon a plate movements so rapid, that, in reality, they occupy an inconceivable fraction of a second. The rider at full speed seems arrested, in order to be pictured. So to God, not only the acts of every instant, even of the most minute fraction of a second, are known, but the entire process in its whole extent is displayed. From all eternity, God knows in whom His regenerating grace would reach its intended result, and among whom it would encounter that prolonged resistance which it is not His will to remove. God, from all eternity, has known those who are His.

The Plan of Redemption thus provided, was not one in which mercy was to be exercised at the expense of justice. Every punishment which justice would impose must be inflicted. Not the least burden the Law required could be removed. Sin had been committed, and the penalty of sin in its fullest extent had to be paid. This penalty could neither be extinguished nor commuted. Eternal death, and nothing less, is the wages of sin. Man could be delivered only after he, or else after someone for him, would suffer eternal death. But when could a finite creature ever discharge an infinite obligation? Were all good angels and archangels to combine in an effort to pay the penalty which but one member of the human race had merited, they would only be offsetting an infinite debt by a finite payment.

If, however, an infinite debt was to be paid, how could the Infinite enter into the sphere of the finite, so as to be able to pay a debt? How could the Immutable suffer? How could the Immortal die? It is useless to speculate as to whether any other mode were possible. It is enough to trace the plan adopted by God, rather than to waste time and energy in attempting to prove that even God could not devise another. The plan devised and clearly described in the New Testament is one by which the Son of God, co-equal and co-eternal with the Father, assumed the human nature into the unity of His person. From the moment of His conception by the Holy Ghost, of the Virgin Mary, the person forever had two natures inseparably united; so that the person could suffer and die in His human nature, which was ever sustained under the aggregation of the sins of the world, by all the infinite power and merit of the divine nature. The infinite obligation of man was thus discharged, and at the same time infinite merit procured for man. The work of man's divinely-human substitute was thus to be accounted as though it had actually been wrought by man himself.

This plan which was executed in time was in God's purpose from all eternity. Christ was thus the Lamb slain from the foundation of the world; i.e., because His sacrifice for man's sin was eternally foreknown, and eternally taken into the account in God's estimate of man. But this plan, as devised from Eternity, was occupied not simply with the procuring of Redemption, but also with the application of it. Even then, while God was reconciled to all men in Christ, He was reconciled to none outside of Christ. All were forgiven in Christ; none were forgiven outside of Christ. That Redemption should be realized, those for whom it was intended had to be brought to such relation to Christ, that they could be said to be "in Christ." A series of agencies for applying Redemption, or bringing Christ to men, and men to Christ, is, therefore, also devised. The gift of the Holy Spirit, the efficiency of the Holy Spirit in the means of grace, the various stages of His applying work, until Redemption would reach its goal in life eternal, all were comprehended in the plan. Whatever result of divine grace was reached in time, belonged to God's Eternal Purpose. Every step in the calling, illumination, regeneration, justification, sanctification and glorification of believers—the entire positive side of every Christian life, from the first approach of the means of grace to it, until the hour of death, the entrance into another world, the resurrection of the dead, the Judgment Day, and the session with the Lord in glory, occurs as each was foreordained from Eternity, and as the result of this foreordination. Every saving act of God, for and in, and through us, comes from this source. There is a stream bearing the child of God onward with ever increasing volume and force, which rises far distant in the infinite heights of God's love, and is lost again in the ocean of indescribable glory and happiness, which is its goal. In this sense, it is just as true that men are elected to faith, as that they are elected to salvation; for all that is of God in the application of Redemption, is the fruit of God's election.

But God's purpose has nothing to do with the unbelief and resistance, the sin and condemnation of men. God's Eternal Plan of Redemption has to do with the salvation, and not with the destruction of men. It has to do only with the arrest of the processes of corruption that belong to spiritual death. Eternal death is the issue of man's election of sin, and his self-determination to sin. If no soul is saved, except through God's purpose and work, according to this purpose, no soul is lost except by man's own preference for sin. Every resistance of offered grace, every inability to respond to God's call, all apathy with respect to spiritual things, comes from man's own powers, and not from God's purpose. Predestination is not a generic term with two species, one Predestination to Life, known as Election, and the other Predestination to Death, known as Reprobation. All Predestination is also Election. Men are said to be reprobate, only as they are foreseen from Eternity adhering to the Order of Sin and Death, and claiming for themselves the ability— which every man has—to exclude the saving grace of God. Thus, the Scriptural doctrine of Predestination, while claiming for God the sole glory for, and making Him the sole cause of man's salvation, is most carefully guarded from all Fatalism, since every elect and regenerate man could, by his own will, be otherwise than he is, while it is alone by God's will that he is, as he is. If the resistance of God's will, at all times possible in this life, had occurred or would occur, the Divine Omniscience would have recorded it from Eternity, and he would not be numbered among the elect, i.e., those who believe unto the end.

It is in time that this plan of salvation becomes manifest. Every true treatment of God's Eternal Plan must be occupied with the revelation of that plan, and the carrying out of its provisions in time. We learn to know the doctrine of Predestination, not by speculating concerning what may be God's secret will, but by studying His will as manifested in the Gospel. Whatever God determined from all Eternity to do for man's salvation, the Gospel proclaims and declares. The Gospel is not to be interpreted by a doctrine of Predestination, but Predestination is to be interpreted by the Gospel. Every provision of Divine Grace, contained in the Gospel, as proclaimed in time, was in the Divine Plan from all Eternity. If God justifies men in time by faith, He determined from all Eternity, that they should be justified by faith. He elected them from Eternity to be justified and eternally saved by faith. What that means we must learn from the Order of Salvation proclaimed in time. We read God's will in the Gospel, and that is all we need know.

CHAPTER X
PROVIDENCE AND ITS
RELATIONS TO REDEMPTION

WE know of the doctrine of Providence only from the standpoint of Redemption. We have no revelation concerning Providence, apart from the provision which was being made for the carrying out of God's Eternal purposes of love for man. For the center of Providence is man. As all things were created, so all things are preserved for the sake of man, and directed towards the attainment of the end, which, notwithstanding man's departure from the plan which was offered in Creation, is, nevertheless, by Redemption, in store for man.

The very mention of "Preservation" implies the presence of disorganizing and disrupting forces, whose activity must be counteracted. All Creation has been made to suffer for man's sin, and tends of itself to ruin. But a greater power is constantly interposed. One force is balanced by another. An irregularity in one direction corrects an irregularity on the opposite side; and so the frame of Nature stands, as the ground, upon and through which God's power is to work within a higher sphere. Nature is made the servant of Redemption. In all things it is subordinate to the Supernatural, for which it continues to exist. The so-called Laws of Nature are only God's ordinary modes of acting through Nature. To claim that God cannot act otherwise than by them, is to make the Supernatural subordinate to the Natural, or rather to absolutely deny the existence of the Supernatural; and to deny the existence of the Supernatural is to deny the existence of God. The Natural and the Supernatural are not as distant as are often imagined. They refer to God's ordinary and extraordinary, His visible and invisible modes of working. All that is Natural has also a Supernatural side.

More mysterious than God's Preservation is His Concurrence with created things. He lives in all that lives, and acts in all that acts. All energy comes ultimately from God. All motion is not partly from God and partly from the creature, but the activity of God and the creature are one and the same. It is more than a brilliant poetical figure we employ, when the thunder is called the voice of God. He lightens and burns in every flame, rushes forth in every storm, and breathes in every breeze, and blooms in every flower. When I raise my arm or use my pen, God works in and through me, and, in every stroke I make, He makes His presence felt. I can do nothing, in and through which He does not also work.

The greatest difficulty lies in the application of this doctrine to the sinful acts of men. But it vanishes when the distinction is observed, that sin does not lie in the activity of the creature, but in the determination of the activity to a sinful end. The external act of Eve in stretching her hand towards the fruit was not sinful, but the determination of the act to what God had forbidden, was sinful. The act is the same externally, whether as a soldier I slay an enemy of my country in battle, or, as the head of a family, shoot a robber who has broken into my house, or as the victim of fierce passion, murder my friend. The moral quality of the act must be measured by its relation to God's will; and for its determination in that regard, I am responsible. Every creature of God is good; the perversion of the creature to a use God has not sanctioned, is sin. The electricity which permeates a wire is an energy derived from God; but when, by the carelessness of men, it carries with it death, the guilt is man's. The wheels of the locomotive are not responsible for the life of the man who has thrown himself before their resistless progress. Man is responsible for the use of the Divine Energy which God has placed at his disposition. The old scholastic distinction is worthy of being continually employed, that it is not the effect, but the defect in an action that is sin.

If such be God's concurrence, even with what is evil and sinful, His concurrence with what is good is still more marked. All that is good is either God, or from God. His relation with that outside of Himself which is good, is far more than that of concurrence. He is, in the first place, it's Author; and then He concurs with the development of the new endowments, and the exercise of the new powers which He has implanted. All the workings of Divine Grace, although ordinarily referred to another sphere, are, in reality, only forms of Providential control and efficiency. In grace the movements of Providence are specialized and intensified.

God's concurrence with what is good leads it, above all obstacles, to the end which both God and the sanctified creature, by God's inspiration and guidance, have in view. His concurrence, however, with what is evil, overrules the evil, and converts the very energy employed by the creature for the purpose of antagonizing and obstructing His work, into an instrumentality for furthering His higher and vaster plans. Satan prepared his own punishment when he led humanity into sin; since humanity became the instrument for his destruction, (Gen. 3:15). The greater his rage, as the history of the race advanced, the more signal his defeat. The most stupendous error of all was when he put to death God's Son, and thus contributed towards Redemption. The sons of Jacob sold their brother into bondage, and thus provided for him advancement and honor, that he could not otherwise have secured, and by this means, ultimately made themselves his beggars and bondsmen. In selling him to the traders, they sold themselves to him. While the King of Assyria had no other thought in mind, but that of secular dominion, God used him as the rod of His anger upon degenerate Israel (Isa. 10:5-7). Even the most insignificant events of life have thus far-reaching consequences. Saul went out to seek donkeys, and found a kingdom (1 Sam. 9). The disturbed sleep of Ahasuerus (and this may have come from the buzzing of a gnat) brings salvation to the Jews, and a change in the ministry of his empire. All events are connected with one another by a hidden chain. God's purposes admit of human freedom, and take all the foreseen determinations of that freedom into the account, just as the builder selects different materials for a work which he projects. As from diverse colored stones the skillful artist will make mosaics that have the finish of elaborate paintings, so God uses for His designs, the diversified and seemingly antagonistic elements contributed by human freedom. Not a sparrow falls to the ground without God's notice; not a life—not even that of the most obscure and unnoticed of His creatures—is without its use in contributing to the advancement of His cause. "Man's goings are of the Lord; how then can a man understand his own way?" (Prov. 20:24). One plan rules the world, and everything in the world belongs to that plan, as every note in the orchestra is a factor in the transport of the audience with which the rendering of some masterpiece of a great composer is greeted, or every stroke of the pencil has its effect upon the excellence of the work of a great painter. As the discords in music only make its harmonies the more conspicuous, so sin and death subserve the interests of Holiness, and Life, and Love. "We can do nothing against the truth, but for the truth." (2 Cor. 13:8).

This implies that, for the attainment of His purposes, God is constantly employing second causes. It is God's plan to use means for the purpose of working out His places. The only answer we can give to the question why He does not act directly and immediately, is that it is not His will, ordinarily, so to work. Every object of Creation is a factor in the great world problem. Irrational creatures and inanimate Nature have in it their place. So also, the higher order of creatures, the angels, created above man, but destined to be overtaken and surpassed by man in the development of the new life introduced into humanity by Redemption. The agency of angels in administering "to the heirs of salvation," and thus to the attainment of God's purposes with respect to this world, is a doctrine most clearly taught, although the extent of this administration is not known. That through their invisible service, just as through man's visible service, effects are wrought, for the advancement of God's Kingdom, upon the external world, as well as within the sphere of spiritual influence, is not a matter of speculation, but of clear revelation. We see and know only so much of the agencies employed by God, as is necessary for our fulfillment of the part assigned us. The soldier in an army, making a victorious advance, need not know the details that are being wrought out by his general, with respect to the complicated provisions that must be made to move with rapidity and success the hundreds of thousands of men whom he commands. It is enough for him to be acquainted with the recurring duties of every hour, and of every new post into which he has been brought through the will of his commander, communicated through a series of officers that intervene.

Nor does God's ordinary employment of second causes in any way contradict the possibility or fact of His occasional immediate activity. God is not bound to second causes. They are simply His servants. What He does through creatures, He can do, just as well and as readily, without creatures. Nor does He confine Himself to but one way of working through them. He may work through them more rapidly or more slowly; He may accelerate or retard the effects. The production of wine at Cana was in itself no more wonderful than what God does yearly in the laboratory of the vineyards. The miracle consisted in the fact that what is in other cases accomplished by a long process, some of whose details men have learned, was then accomplished very quickly, and without those links through which God ordinarily works. He who called creatures out of nothing, and arranged a series of second causes through which wine is made from water, as it passes through the ground, the roots and branches, the buds and blossoms and clusters of the vine, the processes of compression, fermentation, etc., could just as readily make wine out of nothing, as He made it out of the fruit of the vine. A slight variation in the laws of refraction, or the passage of the sun's rays through a medium of slightly different density, would keep the sun above the horizon, so as to partially explain Joshua's lengthened day. The water of the river could be made more dense, or the iron could be made lighter, in order to bring the axe to the surface at the command of the prophet. The denial of the reality of the miraculous by those who admit the existence of a personal God, is stranger than any miracle that has ever been wrought.

When the career of a man upon earth has been completed, we can sometimes review the course over which he has passed, and trace with distinctness the various elements that have contributed to the formation of his character and influence. We may even, on rare occasions, go further, and, if the period of survey be sufficiently distant, we can decide to some extent concerning the peculiar office for which God raised him up. In the same way, we may study different schools and tendencies of religious thought, or the development of Christianity, in its varied forms, such as the Greek, the Latin, the Germanic. A still wider view will survey the entire history of the world, and trace, in its entire extent, the development of a Divine purpose, leading towards an end, which, we know from God's Word, is sure to follow.

It belonged to this plan, that God did not immediately execute His sentence of death upon man. Instead of personally uniting Himself with one of Adam's immediate sons, he left humanity to struggle with sin for many generations, sustained by the hope of a coming Deliverer, and, in its struggle, developing all the capacities of humanity for the reception of the promised Salvation. All the crimes and vices of a world without God were overruled and utilized in the preparation of Redemption. Thus in Heathenism, man was prepared for salvation, while in Judaism salvation was prepared for man. Everything tended towards the dispensation of the fullness of the times, Eph. 1:10; Gal. 4:4. There is a vast receptacle to which every year and every century and every millennium has poured its streams, until the last limit of its capacity is reached; all is full and fulfilled. This explains every critical point in the history of an individual, and of a Nation, and of a Church communion and of the world. The two main crises in the history of the world are those which mark the completion of Redemption, and the completion of the application of Redemption. Both the first and the second coming of Christ are the Fullness of the Times. This entire world's history is a history of Redemption.

We may instance the preparation of the Greek language, as the instrument through which the truths of revelation were to be most fully recorded, as a particular example of Providential guidance working through men entirely unconscious of the process. Each era of its literature contributed new elements, until at last when it had become the language of the world, the mold was ready in which the Divine contents of revelation were cast. The New Testament could never have been written in the vocabulary of Homer. The great epic poet furnished the language for the description of scenery, and the vivid recital of events. The tragedians developed the Greek language as a vehicle for describing deep emotion. The great philosophers, Plato and Aristotle, cultivated its adaptation to the analysis of human thought, and the purposes of generalization and classification. Thus the language was ready, when the civilized world was not only of one speech, but also was under one government, and connected by a network of great roads, making intercourse between distant points frequent and easy.

A similar preparation for the spread of the Reformation might be noted, in the Fall of Constantinople, the dispersion of learned Greeks into the Christian centers of Europe, the consequent revival of learning and new attention to classical studies, leading inevitably to more close attention to the original languages of the Holy Scriptures. With this was combined the impulse imparted by geographical extension, as the result of the discovery of America, and the new hopes of future progress which were inspired. There is no true Philosophy of History, except one that is occupied in tracing the Hand of God, beneath all human events. Such a philosophy we find outlined already in Daniel 2:31-45, where the Assyrio-Babylonian, Medo-Persian, Macedonian and Roman World Empires are described as succumbing before the power of the world-empire of a diverse kind that was to rise from an obscure source and oppose them.

CHAPTER XI
THE ONE PERSON AND THE TWO NATURES

"WHEN the fullness of the time was come, God sent forth His Son, made of a woman, made under the law, to redeem them that were under the law" (Gal. 4:4-5). This was the mystery, hidden from the beginning in God, which was at length revealed in Christ (Eph. 3:9). Not in an obscure time and place, but at the best known period of the Ancient World, and in a land which still retains the peculiarities of that period, did the Son of God take upon Himself man's nature. The geographical and historical background of those eventful years are clearly portrayed on the pages of contemporary writers, who cannot be charged with prejudices in favor of Christianity. So well-established are the facts that the leading nations of the world make them the starting-point for their chronological reckoning. Jesus of Nazareth is proved to be the Son of God and the promised Messiah, by the fulfillment in Him of the prophecies of the Old Testament. Such was

His own claim, which He asked to have tested when He said: "Search" (or "ye search") "the Scriptures; they are they which testify of Me," John 5:39. "To Him, whom they slew and hanged on a tree," whom "God raised up the third day," "gave all the prophets witness" That these prophecies of the Old Testament were fulfilled in Him is the main argument of the New Testament.

Jesus is his personal name, by which he was distinguished from other men; Christ or Messiah is his official name. His personal name was one of the most common among the Jews. It is the same as Joshua; but as applied to Jesus of Nazareth, it has a new significance. Christ, the official name, does not properly belong to the Son of God, until he has assumed human flesh. In Christ, the divine and human are forever and inseparably united. He was the Christ, neither in his divine nature alone, nor in his human nature alone, but in these two natures together, each of them acting according to its peculiarities in the execution of the Messianic office.

The incarnation of the Son of God, is the mystery of all mysteries, above and beyond all thought. All that revelation teaches, only removes the difficulties concerning it further back, but affords no explanation. To the last, it remains an article of faith, to be believed, but not to be understood. A few days before his death, Melanchthon enumerated in parallel columns the negative and the positive advantages of a departure from this life, and reached the culmination of the latter when he wrote: "You will learn the wonderful mystery you could not understand in this life, how the two natures in Christ are united." But even then, the fact will only be the more vividly presented; mystery upon mystery will continue to rise upon us as we con template it.

The finite can never contain the Infinite. How the Infinite could be personally united to the finite, so as to be subject to its limitations, is the problem our utmost reasoning cannot solve. The exaltation of such truths above the highest stretch of thought, only proves, instead of disproves, that Christianity is the revelation of an Infinite God. For what is no higher than finite thought, must be of finite origin. In considering the incarnation, we must be satisfied with the *that*; we are not to be concerned about the *how*. We are always to remember that we cannot go beyond what God has revealed.

From this revelation, it is certain that there is in Christ but one person. Otherwise there would be no incarnation. It was the Eternal Word, who from the beginning was with God, and was God, and by whom all things were made, who was made flesh and dwelt among men. A man speaking with truly human lips could say: "I and my Father are one;" "He that hath seen me hath seen the Father." The arguments upon which the proof of the divinity of the Second Person of the Trinity depends, are composed largely of passages in which a man receives Divine names and proclaims his title to Divine honor and glory.

No new personality, therefore, originated with the conception and birth of Jesus. This distinguishes His birth from that of all other men. Their birth means the existence of a person that before had no existence, or that had potential existence only, according to the principle of heredity. But when Jesus was born, the Person was that of the Eternal Son of God. If it had been otherwise, we would find in Jesus of Nazareth, two persons, a Divine from all eternity, and a human dating with the beginning of his earthly course. As there are not two persons, the Person comes entirely from the divine nature. The Incarnation occurred by the Son of God taking upon Himself a human nature, i.e., by taking upon Himself everything essential to human nature, except that which took upon itself the human nature, viz.: the inner and determining. A human nature, it is true, cannot exist without personality. But the human nature of Christ never was without personality. It's distinguishing feature, however, was that it had no personality of its own. Its personality was that of the divine nature, for personalized human nature did not first come into existence; and the divine nature then assume it. But the human nature came into personalized existence by the very act of the Divine Person by which He took humanity into union with Himself. The Son of God did not unite Himself with a human person, but with a human nature. Christ's humanity is, in all respects, the same as ours, except in that, which would carry with it the denial of the Son of God having become truly man.

The Divine Person of Christ was thus always that which acted; the natures, divine and human, unchanged, unconfused, indivisible and inseparable, the means through which the Divine Person acted. There was no substitution of the one nature for a portion of the other; as though, e.g., the divine nature replaced the human spirit or the human will. He was "truly God and truly man, of a reasonable soul and body; consubstantial with the Father according to the Godhead, and consubstantial with us according to the Manhood" (Athanasian Creed). The natures were so inseparably united, that, to all Eternity, wherever the one nature is, there also is the other. While unconfused, they are at the same time inseparable. It is not, however, any confusion, when it is maintained that the union of these two natures is such, that the one acts upon and affects the other, and qualities of one nature are imparted to the other. Soul and body are not confused; and yet the soul, by its presence within the body, animates it, and gives to the body certain of the qualities of the soul. The wire is no less truly iron, or copper, when charged with an electric current, or aglow with heat. Believing men become, in a certain sense, partakers of the divine nature, 2 Peter 1:4. Much more does that human nature, in which a Divine Person dwells. The Divine Person pervades the human nature, which He has inseparably united with Himself, and imparts to the human nature His attributes; for the Divine Person can in no way be separated from the divine nature. Man always remains man, but he is to all Eternity man endowed with all the power and wisdom and glory of God. The attributes of God can be lacking in man personally united with God, only if the Divine Person could be conceived of as abandoning the humanity which He had assumed. But the humanity having no personality but that of the divine nature, a break in the personal union, would leave humanity without personality; and, without personality, no human life can exist. The doctrine of the impartation of attributes is, therefore, essential to that of the personal union.

CHAPTER XII
THE STATE OF HUMILIATION

WHEN the Son of God became man, there was no abandonment upon His part of His rule over the Universe, until the salvation of those whom He had chosen would be completed; the doctrine of the Trinity at once forbids us to conceive of two of the Persons exercising the prerogatives of God apart from the other. He was upholding all things by the Word of His power, even while He was the Babe of Bethlehem. But, until Redemption was complete, the Divine Person, in the administration of His Kingdom of Power, did not act ordinarily through His human nature. Through the personal union, the human nature participated in the divine attributes, but did not avail itself of them. The Divine Person abstained in His human nature from their full use. This explains the so-called State of Humiliation. God could not, in His own nature, be humiliated or "emptied." An infinite nature admits of nothing either higher or lower. But by assuming a human nature, the Divine Person may be humiliated in that nature. The human nature having all the attributes of the divine communicated to it, is humiliated or "emptied," when this nature does not fully employ these gifts. Our Lord in His humanity could have demanded all the honor and glory that belong to God; for God would have then only claimed for Himself His due. But in not making this claim, and in not employing, in His humanity, these attributes, and in permitting Himself to be accounted no more than any other man, and thus submitting to the form of a servant, consisted His humiliation, Phil. 2:5-9.

This humiliation had its degrees. The word "full" is used advisedly, when Christ is said to have abstained from the full use of the communicated attributes. Every miracle which Christ wrought was through His use of these attributes. When He told of the death of Lazarus, and gave directions concerning His triumphal entry and the first Lord's Supper, He exercised His Omniscience; but He abstained from its exercise when He declared His ignorance of the day and hour of His second coming, Mark 13:32. When a single word from His mouth prostrated the armed men sent to arrest Him, John 18:6, He exercised His Omnipotence, but immediately refraining from its exercise, He was arrested and bound. The Humiliation was necessary, in order that the price for man's sin might be paid. Glimpses of His divine power and glory flashed forth from the darkness, in order that, even amidst the deepest humiliation, the eye of faith might discern what the lips joyfully confessed: "This is none other than the Son of God."

The State of Exaltation is the period when the Divinely-human Person exercises the divine attributes through the human, as well as through the divine nature; in other words, when the humanity freely uses the communicated divine attributes. It may be a question as to whether it be proper to say that the humanity always fully exercised them, even then; for there are degrees in Exaltation as in Humiliation. There are limitations self-imposed upon the humanity of Christ, even subsequent to the Resurrection. There is a progress from the post-resurrection to the post ascension period; and even now, although His humanity reign at the Right Hand of God, a still higher stage is in prospect, "when He shall have put down all rule and all authority and power," 1 Cor. 15:24.

Such is the doctrine of the Communication of Attributes, as explained by the Gospel record of our Lord's Humiliation and Exaltation. The Son of God was not humiliated by His incarnation; for since the State of Humiliation is over, He remains, in the State of Exaltation, incarnate. But He was humiliated by the mode and conditions, in which He became incarnate and lived incarnate.

The force of the entire doctrine bears upon the fact that, in all His official acts as Redeemer, the Divine Person acts through both natures. He paid the price of man's redemption in His human nature; for the divine nature could not be subject to the Law, or suffer and die. His divine imparted to the human strength to accomplish all that the Law demanded, and to sustain the accumulated guilt of the world, (for any merely human nature would have sunk under the weight). It gave to His fulfillment of the Law infinite merit. Without this impartation of divine properties to the human nature, Redemption would have been impossible. All who hold to the efficacy of the vicarious sufferings of Christ believe in some mode of Communication of Attributes, even when their language seems to most decidedly reject it.

With this relation of the two natures made clear, we are prepared to consider the various stages of Humiliation and Exaltation. The Humiliation began with the conception by the Holy Ghost. The *Te Deum* expresses this correctly in the original, and as used in English by the Church of England: "When Thou tookest upon Thee to deliver man, Thou didst not abhor the Virgin's womb." It was a true conception that there occurred; the body of Mary was not simply the channel through which a pre-existent humanity descended from Heaven and was introduced to earth. Nor was there a new creation of humanity within the womb of Mary. "God sent forth His Son, made of a woman," Gal. 4:4. The humanity of Mary was the source of Christ's humanity. Otherwise the emphasis laid by the evangelists upon the genealogical tables would be inexplicable. He was made of the seed of David, according to the flesh, Roman 1:3. The miraculous element in our Lord's conception lies in the mode in which a separate human life emerges from that of the mother. The ordinary course of Nature is replaced by a special act of God, not, indeed, by creation, but, by a direct divine influence, supplying the principle of life lying dormant within her, with that impulse and those capacities for separate growth that under other circumstances, require the agency of man.[1]

The Humiliation of Christ is manifest here in the fact, that while He might have become incarnate in the full glory with which He will return to judgment, or in the full growth and vigor with which Adam was endowed in Eden, He enters

---

[1] See Augsburg Confession, Art. III.

the world just as other men. He became not simply a feeble infant, but, far less than an infant, the Son of God was borne about by Mary for the usual period of pre-natal existence. Thus He became the Son of Mary, just as truly as He became man; and Mary, while not the mother of the divine nature, yet, by becoming the mother of the Person inseparably united with the humanity derived from her, became the mother of God. She could not be the mother of the humanity without also being the mother of the person; humanity cannot exist without a person. The relationship between mother and child is one of person to person, and not simply of nature to nature. Mary, therefore, as a person, having a relation to Jesus as a person, is truly the mother of Jesus. But the person of Jesus is that of the Son of God, co-equal and co-eternal God, consubstantial with the Father from all eternity. Such was the main point which the Church had to assert and define against the Nestorians in the Fifth Century, as the Council of Chalcedon declared: "Born of the Virgin Mary, the Mother of God, according to the manhood."

The Holy Scriptures give us no warrant for teaching a miraculous birth of Christ except as it was the issue of the miraculous conception. The miracle lies in the union of divinity with humanity within the womb of Mary. When that union is formed, it belongs to the Humiliation of Christ, that the natural, endowed with supernatural powers, should grow according to the limitations of the natural. With the attributes imparted to the human nature from the first moment of the conception, the Lord at any moment, during His prenatal state, could have left His mother and appeared as a teacher in Jerusalem, or as a conqueror to His downtrodden race. But this would not have been consistent with His humiliation. In the State of Humiliation, except only on rare occasions, everything follows the order of natural growth. So in all the developments of God's plans in His Kingdom. The supernatural or miraculous enters simply as the beginning of a new development. Christ could have come forth from His mother, as He passed through the closed doors after His resurrection; but to affirm that He did so, fails to distinguish between the States of Humiliation and Exaltation. Being made "in the likeness of man," implies that His birth was a true birth, and not, as is the usual doctrine of Medieval theologians, the mere appearance of a birth.

It seems scarcely necessary, from a standpoint which accepts the divinity of Christ as a matter that is raised above all controversy to enter into any argument concerning the sinlessness of Christ, distinguishing His conception and birth from that of all other men. Sin is a personal matter. It does not belong to a nature apart from the person. Human nature is sinful, only as it is regarded as the aggregate of human personalities. But the Person of Christ is that of His divine nature. To say that a Divine Person sins is a contradiction; for sin is nothing but a want of conformity with the divine will. Whatever God wills is the standard of holiness. The very fact of incarnation declares the complete pervasion and possession of the human nature by the divine, so that the human will in Him is even more entirely responsive to the divine will, than our bodies are to the dictates of our human wills. The absence of Original Sin in Him is to be explained, not so much by a special sanctification of the nature in Mary, as by the fact that the personality in Christ is supplied by the divine and not by the human nature. The Holy One was the Son of God inhabiting a nature which personally united to Himself could not be other than holy. Every defect, weakness and perversity of the nature in body and soul, descending by heredity from parent to child, were removed and more than counter balanced by the indwelling of God. New divine powers even then pervaded it by reason of the personal union. Christ was not only sinless. He was absolutely impeccable. His temptation in no way involves the possibility of a fall. We associate temptation with peccability, because that is our experience. But this is not involved necessarily in temptation or trial. Gold is brought to the touch stone to be tested, but this does not imply that there is any possibility of real gold being found to be a counterfeit. Temptation only brings to view what has hitherto been obscure. The agony of our Lord under temptation, did not arise from any apprehensions on His part of a fall. He knew all the while that He would not yield to sin, and the tempter would be conquered. The agony is explained by the fact that the temptation was part of His Passion.

The life of Christ progressed on earth. "Jesus increased in wisdom and stature, and in favor with God and man," Luke 2:52. The Humiliation involving the almost complete abstaining from the use of the imparted divine gifts, His humanity admitted of and received the same development as that of other children. The divine attributes unused, He is, in His humanity, a perfect, but at the same time a finite and an undeveloped man. He passed through all the stages of human life, exhibiting each stage in its highest perfection. It was a growth from grace to grace, a part of that obedience by which many were made righteous. He was obedient to all the demands of the Law, and perfectly fulfilled it. He endured all the penalties awaiting the whole race for whose salvation He intervened.

The suffering of Christ began with His birth. His parents were poor; He was born, almost as an outcast, among cattle. On the eighth day He shed first His blood, in the ordinance of circumcision. To avoid Herod, He was carried into Egypt. A general massacre of the infants of Bethlehem was made, in order that the godless ruler might be sure that He had not escaped. The sufferings grew as His life advanced. They were only, in small part, physical. The heaviest burdens came from the ingratitude and rejection of men, the subjection to the suggestions and insults of Satan, and the consciousness of being charged with the accumulated guilt of the world, and thus being, for the time, in God's sight, the culprit of all culprits the world has ever known. The blows, the scourge, the crown of thorns, the faded, cast-off cloak, the defilement of His cheeks with the spittle of coarse men, the nailing to the cross, the raging fever that followed with its violent thirst, were nothing compared with the pain the shouts of "crucify Him," and "not this man, but Barrabas," occasioned, and that broke His heart while He uttered the cry, "My God, why hast Thou forsaken Me?", "He became obedient to death, even the death of the cross," Phil. 2:8. By the words: "It is finished," John 19:30, He proclaimed that provision had at last been made for every sin, that there was nothing more for Him or for any soul whom He redeemed, to pay as a satisfaction for sin. The burial is not so much another stage in the State of Humiliation, as it is an attestation of the reality of His death.

CHAPTER XIII
THE STATE OF EXALTATION

The Descent into Hell belongs, not to the State of Humiliation, but to that of Exaltation. Acts 2:27, contains no reference to the descent and, as the original shows, does not declare that the soul of Christ was actually in Hell. The doctrine rests upon 1 Pet. 3:18-19. The contrast there between "flesh" and "spirit" is precisely the same as in Rom. 1:3-4, the one referring to the human, and the other to the divine nature. The descent follows the quickening, and was therefore one that was made both in body and in soul. It was an act of Christ in His reanimated body. The spirits to whom He preached were "in prison." This may be understood by the reference to the fallen angels in 2 Pet. 2:4; Jude 6. The Antedeluvians are especially mentioned as types of notorious and flagrant transgressors, who reviled Noah when he preached of righteousness, just as contemporaries of Peter were ridiculing the warnings of approaching judgment uttered by Christian preachers, 2 Pet. 3:3-4. As the preaching of Noah, after many ages, was vindicated at the Descent of Christ and His preaching to the spirits in prison, so the Christians of his day would in ages to come be vindicated at Christ's Second Coming. The underlying thought is: "Be patient. The men of to-day may scorn you as visionaries, because of your preaching. So Noah was despised. But those who despised him were terrified to learn, in the eternal world, from the lips of the Lord, that all that Noah proclaimed was certainly to be fulfilled."

There is not the least intimation given in the passage concerning any preaching of repentance or forgiveness, or any preaching of the Gospel. The word used is indeterminate, meaning simply "to herald forth," "to proclaim." No other passage of Scripture allows us to read this as a preaching of the Gospel, 1 Pet. 4:6, sometimes so interpreted, refers not to a preaching of the Gospel to the dead while dead, but to a former preaching to those now dead while they were living; just as in the preceding verse, the judging of "the quick and the dead," cannot refer to a judging of the dead while dead, but looks forward to the Judgment Day, when those who are now dead will be raised, and "the quick and the dead" will both be alike alive before God's bar. The whole tenor of Scripture being to the effect that there will be no place of repentance hereafter to those who have despised the preaching of the Gospel in this life, we are forced to the conclusion that this passage refers to a triumph of Christ over His enemies. Those who object to this, as though it were derogatory to Christ's character, otherwise so mild and tender towards sinners, forget that the State of Exaltation marks another treatment of those persistently impenitent. The same Lord who weeps over sinners in the State of Humiliation, will dash them in pieces, like a potter's vessel, in the day of His wrath, Ps. 2:9. The Lamb of God is also the Lion of the tribe of Judah Rev. 5:5, and the prayer is recorded of those who implore the rocks and mountains to fall upon them, and hide them from the wrath of the Lamb, Rev. 6:16.

In the absence of any revelation concerning it, it is a matter of surmise which may be cherished as of great probability, that, according to the view long current in the Church, the same announcement of completed Redemption which struck terror into the condemned, was heard also to the joy of the Patriarchs of the Old Testament, who lived in hope of the promised Messiah, but had died without the sight. If He manifested Himself to the one class to their terror, would it not be just like what we know of Him, while visibly among men, to have gladdened the other class with the anticipation of their future glory, resting upon the assurance that their redemption is now complete?

The Resurrection was a proof of the completion of Redemption so strong and manifest, that, in the book of Acts and in the Epistles, it is dwelt upon more frequently and emphatically than even His death. "Who was delivered for our offences, and was raised again for our justification," (Rom. 4:25). The Resurrection declared that, although the burden of the sins of the world rested upon Christ, they were unable to hold Him within the realm of death and the grave. He rose above them all. Every item of the world's indebtedness was fully paid, and there is nothing more that death can claim, either of Him or of those who are found in Him. The righteousness that avails before God for the believer, rises, like a lofty mountain, from the swelling flood of the world's sins that rage around it, and for many fathoms have hidden it from view. The death of Christ brings us comfort only as it is contemplated in the light of the Resurrection, and, when, with the Apostle, we exclaim: "Who is He that condemns? It is Christ that died, yea, rather that is risen again."

With the *descensus*, the Resurrection marks the beginning of the positive, the active, the aggressive side of Christ's work. The State of Humiliation marks the passive side. On the Cross, Satan was permitted to do his worst. Our Lord submitted himself to the power of death, and yielded up His spirit. In the Resurrection, the case is reversed. Satan's weapons have been exhausted, and Christ now turns upon him. A mightier Samson brings down with his nod the pillars of the prison within which he has been placed, but, unlike Samson, rises unharmed from the ruins, while the prisoners escape. "Through death," because, if there had been no death, there would have been no resurrection, He destroys "him that had the power of death and delivers them who through fear of death were all their life time subject to bondage," Heb. 2:14. There is no longer any sting to death; or any victory for the grave. Whenever oppressed by the terrors of death, we need only go, with our adversary to the empty tomb, and say to him: "Look there. You have exhausted your power on my substitute, and there is no more you can do. He is risen and I am free. Christ will use death as His slave to bring me to His presence, but except as Christ's slave, death has nothing, and can have nothing to do with me. Christ has risen, and with Him, I have risen to a new life." It is the resistless life of God, triumphing over human sin and human weakness, that the Resurrection shows, a life which goes forth to impart a Resurrection-power to all who by faith enter into life-communions with Christ, Rom. 6:8-11. The secret of the aggressive force of the Apostolic Church which rendered it unwearied by the fatigues, and undeterred by the dangers and sacrifices of its missionary enterprises, lay largely in the vividness of its conception of the reality of the Resurrection. All the Apostolic teaching was concentrated in their commission to be witnesses of the Resurrection, Acts 1:22. The rising of their Master from the depth of His humiliation, to attack His great enemy, inspired them with courage and enthusiasm to wage an active war against him, wherever traces of his presence could be found on earth. They went forth with no uncertainty as to the issue; for they contended against an opponent already overthrown and conquered. They knew that within them dwelt and wrought the very life that the grave could not restrain, Rom. 8:11; Gal. 2:20, and this rendered those otherwise most timid, bold in proclaiming the cause of Christ, and advancing His Kingdom, Acts 4:33. The greatest remedy for indifference and lack of courage to do and bear for Christ, is "to know the power of Christ's Resurrection," Phil. 3:10.

The Resurrection not only makes this argument to the believer, but it presents, against the doubts of skeptics and the rage of the world, the most effectual proof of the Divinity of Christ, Rom. 1:4. It is the miracle above all other miracles. As long as its reality remains undisputed, all doubts concerning other miracles are in vain. It contains and explains all. Appealing, as Christ did, to this miracle, as the test of the truth of His professions, even though He were raised, not by His own power, John 10:18, but by divine power, like that with which He raised others during His ministry, the argument would be overwhelming. God would not honor an impostor thus. Its force was felt not only by believers, but by unbelievers. It was this argument which, in the very city where it occurred, and within a few weeks afterwards, overwhelmed the thousands with confusion on the Day of Pentecost. The testimonies to this fact that made the Apostles aggressive, disheartened and terrified their opponents.

The narrative of the Resurrection shows clearly that the State of Exaltation, like that of Humiliation, had its stages. Even when death is conquered, our Lord does not immediately assume the use of all the attributes imparted to the human nature. He could have come forth from the sealed tomb as readily as He entered the room where the doors were closed, John 20:19. The stone would have been no barrier to a resurrection-body endowed with divinity. But for a while some of the limitations of the State of Humiliation continue, in order to afford the surest proof that the Resurrection was a reality that could be tested by sight and touch. There was an accommodation of the Lord to those whom He purposed, by many infallible proofs, to convince that the very body that had been crucified, and been laid in the grave, had been restored to life. The resurrection-body, handled and felt by the disciples, 1 John 1:1; John 20:27, had new spiritual properties, after which the resurrection- bodies of believers are to be fashioned, Phil. 3:21. But, beside this, it had also properties ordinarily unused, which belonged to it as the abode, in a special manner, of the Second Person of the Trinity.

The Ascension was His formal entrance into His invisible glory. His body, still partaking of some of the limitations of His Humiliation, was localized when He rose from the earth, until a cloud received Him out of sight, (Acts 1:9). A higher stage of Exaltation was reached when "He ascended up far above all heavens, that He might fill all things," Eph. 4:10. His Ascension is the ground of the potential multipresence of His body. He can be wherever He wills to be, in body, as well as in His human spirit. Whether this is explained by its cotemporaneous presence in different places at the same time, or by movements so rapid that the human mind cannot appreciate them, it is not for us to determine. Science which can devise instruments that permanently fix upon paper in an infinitestimal part of a second, the attitude of a rider who is passing before the camera at the rate of less than three minutes per mile, should refrain from questioning the possibilities of a body in which God dwells. The astonishing feats performed, in recent years, by the application of electricity in overcoming distances, and bringing continents together, should start the thought that we may be only at the beginning of discoveries concerning finite and physical things that may lead to yet deeper problems, and humble us thoroughly concerning our disbelief as to what God is able to do. It is enough for us to know that Christ is present in His humanity, as well as in His divinity, wherever He has promised to be. The mode in which this can occur we leave, if we be wise, to the divine Omniscience.

The goal of the Ascension is the Right Hand of God. It seems strange that this ever could have been conceived of as a determinative locality. The imagery of Scripture ought to be plain; for God is a spirit, and is above all localization. As His eye and His ear represent His Omniscience, so His Right Hand represents His Power and Majesty. The Psalms are especially rich in passages speaking of the Lord's "Hand." It only requires an examination to determine their meaning: Ps. 10:12; 21:8; 28:5; 31:5; 31:15; 32:4; 37:24; 38:2; 74:11, etc. Still more expressive is the "Right Hand": Ps. 16:11; 17:7; 18:35; 20:6; 44:3; 45:4; 60:5, etc., especially Ps. 118:15-16. In Ps.

139:10, the Right Hand of God is expressly said to be Omnipresent. When Christ, therefore, is said to sit at the Right Hand of God, nothing more is meant than that the human nature of Christ shares with the divine, the dominion over all things, not simply by possession, but also in use. The same thought is expressed by Stephen in Acts 7:56, by "standing at the Right Hand of God," with the additional idea of the Lord's attention as directed to His struggling people on earth, and of the intercession for them which He makes.

CHAPTER XIV
THE OFFICES OF CHRIST

THE work of Christ for man in his Divinely-human-Person, and in the two states in which it has existed, is comprised in His three offices of Prophet, Priest and King.

Prophet means a proclaimer, one who speaks forth, not simply one who foretells. As Prophet, Christ was "the teacher sent from God," John 3:2, to reveal the will of the Father. From the open heavens, came the voice: "Hear ye him," Matt. 17:5. He was the incarnate Word of God. He came to declare that which no man could know or tell, except as He would make it known. "The only begotten Son, which is in the bosom of the Father, He hath declared him," John 1:18. So exclusively is He the teacher of divine things, that Peter exclaimed: "Lord, to whom shall we go? You have the words of Eternal Life," John 6:69. If there is no certainty in Christ's words, there is certainty nowhere. His teaching was absolutely infallible. In vain, men plead the limitations of the

State of Humiliation, in order to endeavor to prove that, with his refraining from the exercise of the communicated divine knowledge, there was involved the possibility of mistakes. The Revealer of God's will to man made no mistakes; otherwise we would have no trustworthy revelation, and would, after all, be compelled to rest upon mere surmises. No limitations were submitted to by the God-man, except where they were needed for the fulfillment of His office. He humbled himself to be obedient to the Law, to suffer, to die; but not to mislead those who would trust Him as a Divine Teacher. In this, He was illumined with all those riches of Divine Wisdom, which He used and imparted through His words.

In the exercise of this office, He taught the Law, freeing it from the Rabbinical corruptions and additions, with which it had been encumbered, and exhibiting its true spiritual meaning. The Sermon on the Mount is a complete exposition of the Ten Commandments. But His especial work as Prophet was to proclaim the Gospel, i.e., the promise concerning the free forgiveness of sins, to be procured by His work as Priest. This was a new doctrine, differing from that of the Law, not only in degree, but in kind. Obscurely indicated in the Old Testament, only with Him does the actual plan of God for man's salvation become manifest to man. He became thus the great expounder of the Old Testament prophets, showing how all their predictions, which the prophets themselves so little understood when they wrote them, were being fulfilled in the sight of those to whom He preached, Luke 10:24.

His work as a Prophet was not confined to the teaching that fell from His own lips. He commissioned others to proclaim the revelation of God which they had heard of

Him, authenticating their commission with the seal: "He that hears you, hears Me," Luke 10:16. "They went forth and preached everywhere, the Lord working with them," Mark 16:20, claiming to be "ambassadors of Christ," through whom God plead with men, 1 Cor. 5:20, since they taught, as they baptized, not in their own name, but in that of the Holy Trinity, Matt. 28:19. So to the present day, as the message of Christ given to His Apostles is pro claimed by the ministers of the Word, and the Church, Christ is still exercising His office as Prophet through His servants. They are true to their office, only as the voice of Christ sounds forth through them without any human adulterations or additions, or failure to declare all the counsel of God. "If any man speak," whether in the pulpit or through the press, "let him speak as the oracles of God," (1 Peter 4:11). Such is the distinction, made of old, between the immediate and the mediate exercise of the Prophetical Office.

But even in this mediate exercise of the Prophetical Office, the word of man is attended and pervaded by the presence and energizing activity of the Holy Spirit; so that Christ speaks through His ministers, not only by their repetition of what was heard from Him, but because the Spirit itself bears His witness through the Word spoken. Only man seems to speak, but when he speaks what is really the Word of God, its convincing power depends upon the entire Trinity exercising an influence through the Word, far above what the human speaker can ask or think. Christ is still the Prophet wherever the Gospel is proclaimed.

All the work of Christ as a Prophet centers on His office of Priest. As such, He propitiated God by offering a sufficient sacrifice for man's sin, and providing a righteousness of infinite merit. There are two classes of sacrifices mentioned in Holy Scripture, viz., Propitiatory or Expiatory, and Eucharistic. The former render God propitious; the latter are testimonies of thanksgiving. They who offer sacrifices are priests. Eucharistic sacrifices are offered by all believers, who, on this account, are called spiritual priests, 1 Peter 2:5. There is but one propitiatory sacrifice, Christ Himself, the Lamb of God offered for the sins of the world. Hence there is but one real priest, Christ Himself, the sacrifice and the priest being one and the same, Hebrews 4:14; 10:10. The priests and the sacrifices of the Old Testament were not priests and sacrifices in the proper sense. None of their offerings propitiated God, but only announced that a sacrifice was hereafter to be made. They foreshadowed the coming sacrifice, and pointed to Christ, Hebrews 10:1.

This sacrifice Christ made by His voluntary assumption of all the sufferings demanded by the Law, that attended His entire earthly life, from Bethlehem to Calvary. All the acts of the State of Humiliation were sacrificial. All its sufferings were voluntary and cheerful satisfactions offered to God for man's sins. They culminate in the death of Christ. For this reason, the blood of Christ is often mentioned as the price of Redemption, and He is said to have borne our sins upon the Cross, although these declarations do not exhaust the contents of His sufferings. Suffering unto death was the penalty which God had decreed against sin. Suffering and guilt are inseparable. If man was to be freed from guilt, someone must bear his sufferings for him. If he was to be freed from suffering, someone must bear his guilt. Christ took this place. He made Himself chargeable with man's guilt and sin. He became, so far as the Law is concerned, the guilty one that man is, in order that man might be the Holy One that He is, 2 Cor. 5:21. This is the doctrine of the vicarious satisfaction, according to which Christ and man are regarded as exchanging places. He was wounded for our transgressions, He was bruised for our iniquities, the chastisement of our peace was upon Him, and with His stripes we were healed," (Isaiah 53:5).

It is true that the sufferings of Christ exhibit the love of God towards men, and that thus men are moved to repentance; for "God commends His love towards us, in that, while we were yet sinners, Christ died for us," (Romans 5:8). It is true that the sufferings of Christ encourage us to resist sin by the heroic example they afford; for "Christ also suffered for us, leaving us an example," etc., (1 Peter 2:21). It is true that His holiness seen in almost dazzling light amidst the sorrows that overwhelm Him, offers a beginning for that of others whose nature He shares. It is true that the awful penalty he pays divine justice testifies to the earnestness of the divine holiness against sin, in that, when God's own Son took the sinner's place, the punishment laid upon Him was so heavy. It is true, that no preaching so effectually convicts men of sin, as the preaching of the sufferings of Christ, in the light of the Resurrection, Acts 2:23-24. But these were not the main object of Christ's sufferings, which was to be the Lamb of God, to bear the sin of the world.

As eternal death was the punishment decreed against sin, so eternal death was suffered by Christ. Not a stroke less was inflicted than the Law demanded. There was no relaxation or commutation of the penalty. Justice was to be satisfied, and Justice cannot be satisfied with aught less than its "eye for eye, and tooth for tooth." Within the period within which He suffered, His pains were those which all mankind had merited eternally. It was eternal death intensively. Its pains were concentrated within the few years of the Humiliation. The human nature, which suffered was sustained by the infinite strength, and endowed with the infinite merits of the divine nature; and thus the price was paid for the infinite guilt of the race.

Christ did more than suffer for man's sin. Suffering could affect no more than to remove the guilt and penalty. Man stands then where Adam stood when created. But this is only the foundation of his new career. His sins are not only to be forgiven and removed; but there must be positive merit present, which he can offer as his title for Heaven and its blessedness. Besides paying the penalty for sin, Christ, therefore, by His complete obedience to every requirement of the Law, earned for man a righteousness, which is entitled to eternal rewards. Rewards follow obedience, just as certainly as penalties follow disobedience. But these rewards Christ could not receive for Himself, since He is Lord of the Law. Not only was He under no obligation to obey the Law, but His Divine Person is incapable of receiving the merits such obedience brings with it; since the perfection of the Divine cannot be increased. Hence all the rewards belong to those who accept His Salvation. "He was made unto us righteousness," (1 Cor. 1:30). "Christ is the end of the law for righteousness," (Romans 10:4). In Christ, there is provided the inheritance of all things, (1 Cor. 4:22). As He has purchased all men, so also He has purchased for them all things. It must never be forgotten that the righteousness which Christ gives men, is not that which the Divine Person possessed from all eternity, but only that which He earned for men, during His Humiliation, by His perfect compliance with every precept of the Law. "Christ offered to His Heavenly Father, for us poor sinners, His entire, complete obedience, from His holy birth, even unto death" (Formula of Concord, p. 581).

This work of Christ was for all men. None were excepted from it. As universal as is man's sin, just so universal are the provisions for man's redemption. Christ was given for the sins of the world, John 3:16. He tasted death for every man, Heb. 2:9. He died even for those who ultimately perish, Rom. 14:15; Heb. 10:29. The scholastic subtlety that He died sufficiently, but not efficaciously for all, has no warrant in Scripture, which says absolutely and unrestrictedly "He died for all," (2 Cor. 5:15).

Just as clear is it, that He died for all the sins of all men, (1 John 1:7). There is no limitation of the efficacy of His blood to sins committed before baptism, or to original sin. Nor is there anywhere the remotest reference to any commutation of satisfactions which His satisfaction has rendered; so as to bring a penalty, which is utterly beyond man's power to pay, within his ability, and that eternal and infinite, are thus commuted to temporal and finite satisfactions. Christ's satisfaction is entire and complete. All sins are blotted out, or none are blotted out. Where Christ is rejected, there will be no commutation of satisfaction, but even though Christ has died for the sinner, he must endure its full penalty. Where Christ is accepted, there will be no commutation, because man is either altogether forgiven all, or he is forgiven none of his guilt. Forgiveness is a personal matter, and "there is no condemnation to them which are in Christ Jesus," (Romans 8:1). Where guilt is forgiven, all punishments are removed. God never punishes the guiltless; and He never forgives men without regarding them, for Christ's sake, as guiltless. Much less has He any satisfaction to demand of those who are invested with Christ's righteousness, and who thus can lay claim to all the rewards of His meritorious obedience.

Since Christ, by His satisfaction, pays the penalty which was charged against man, and thus provides for his liberation from the guilt and consequences of sin, this work is called Redemption. In some passage of Holy Scripture, the term "redemption" is applied to the full enjoyment of the fruits of this work, as in Luke 21:28; Romans 8:23; Eph. 1:14; 4:30. In this sense, Redemption does not occur until the return of Christ, and the entrance of believers, with body and soul united, into the blessings of Eternal Life. Such redemption is not universal. But, in the more usual sense, Redemption is the act by which the price for man's delivery from sin was paid. Such redemption was universal. The price was paid for all. Even those who ultimately perish were redeemed, Romans 14:15. At the cost of infinite suffering, the prison was reached, the keepers overcome and the doors thrown wide open. Those who decline to avail themselves of the opportunity cannot be said not to have been re deemed. A vast estate has been purchased, and the title freely offered. Those who refuse to accept it cannot complain that they do not enjoy its provisions.

The payment of the satisfaction for sin is a priestly act of Christ that has been completed. There is no further offering for sin, either on the part of men, or of Christ Himself. The Epistle to the Hebrews contrasts the weakness of the Old, with the efficacy of the New Testament, from this very fact. The Old Testament with its frequent sacrifices could not assure the conscience of salvation. Their constant repetition testified to their inadequacy and imperfection. But the efficacy of the New is seen in that Christ "offered one sacrifice for sins forever," Heb. 10:12. It is impossible, therefore, for Him to be offered anew in the Mass, as the Roman Catholic Church teaches.

The payment of the satisfaction for sin is a priestly act of Christ that has been completed. There is no further offering for sin, either on the part of men, or of Christ Himself. The Epistle to the Hebrews contrasts the weakness of the Old, with the efficacy of the New Testament, from this very fact. The Old Testament with its frequent sacrifices could not assure the conscience of salvation. Their constant repetition testified to their inadequacy and imperfection. But the efficacy of the New is seen in that Christ "offered one sacrifice for sins forever," Heb. 10:12. It is impossible, therefore, for Him to be offered anew in the Mass, as the Roman Catholic Church teaches.

There is, however, another priestly act of Christ, which is not completed; but which pertains to the present, as well as to the past, viz., His intercession for believers with the Father, 1 John 2:1; Rom. 8:34; Heb. 7:25; 9:24. This has to do with the application, and not with the procuring of redemption. It Is to be distinguished from the intercession made during His State of Humiliation, as in John 17; Luke 23:34. Into the mysteries of it, we cannot enter It is enough to be comforted by the assurance that in all the trials and dangers of life, the real wants of believers are carried by the Son of God Himself to the Father. This it was that cheered Stephen in his last moments, Acts 7:55.

In considering Christ as a King, it must always be kept in mind that the Regal, like the Prophetical and Priestly functions, has to do entirely with the Mediatorial work. It is that which belongs, therefore, to Christ, as the God-man, and does not comprehend the dominion which pertained to the Second Person of the Trinity before the incarnation. His eternal government is one thing; the participation of the human nature in the government of the world is another. The first part of Hebrews 1:3 refers to a rule of Christ not pertaining to His Kingly office, which the second part of the same verse clearly describes. When the human nature shares with the divine in the sphere of Providence, it is called the Kingdom of Power. But, as all Providence is directed towards the execution of His plans of love in the procuring and application of Redemption, the participation of the human with the divine, in this sphere, is called the administration of the Kingdom of Grace. When the application of Redemption, issues in its full fruition, the Kingdom of Grace passes into that of Glory. They are not in reality different kingdoms, but one and the same kingdom at different stages. The three offices pervade one another. His Kingly office enforces His teaching and renders efficacious His obedience and suffering.

The Kingly office begins with His incarnation. He was born King of the Jews. He received the tributes of a king from the Magi. His kingship was recognized by Nathanael on His entrance upon His ministry, John 1:29. It was proclaimed by the multitudes on the first Palm Sunday. According to the purpose of the Humiliation, He refrained ordinarily from asserting His claims as such, withdrawing Himself from those who desired to publish His kingship, John 6:15. But before Pilate, He asserted His dignity, John 18:37. The superscription over the Cross acknowledged it. But it meant far more than even the disciples imagined. His kingship over Israel was simply the beginning of His Empire. The veil of the temple rent in twain, manifested the extension of His Mediatorial kingdom over all humanity, in fulfillment of Daniel 7:14. In the ascension and session at the right hand of God, He entered upon the still fuller use of His Kingly glory.

Raised "far above all principality and power and might and dominion, and every name that is named, not only in this world, but also in that which is to come," He "put all things under His feet," (Eph. 1:21-22).

His Kingdom is a spiritual Kingdom, which is extended and defended by spiritual means. As John 18:36, declares it is not of this world. Although partially in the world, it is not of the world. Its conquests are not made by the sword. Men use external violence because of their inability to affect their purpose by influencing the heart. Christ, by His Word reaches the heart and wins it, or dispels the plots laid against His Kingdom, as He allayed the violence of winds and waves on Lake Gennesaret.

It is also a Kingdom, which is progressively developed from age to age. We confess this whenever we pray: "Thy Kingdom come." The parable of the mustard-seed and the leaven confirm it. Every century, every generation, every human life, is a separate link in the chain. It has its great epochs, and between these epochs, periods, each with its own peculiarity. Everything looks forward towards the end, when all enemies shall be subdued, and the triumph be complete, (1 Cor. 15:24). The subjection of the Son, of course as man, to the Father, 1 Cor. 15:27, refers to a new mode in which the Kingdom will exist and be administered.

CHAPTER XV
THE KINGDOM OF GOD

Christ has ascended and is seated at the Right Hand of God. A member of the human race is on the Throne of Heaven. All the power of God works through exalted humanity to apply to men forgiveness and righteousness. Redemption is completed, but completed Redemption is to be brought to men, and to develop among them its potencies. The exercise of the Mediatorial Office, begun on earth, is continued in heaven, and, from heaven, directs the entire order of things on earth according to God's eternal plans of redeeming love for the world. The sphere within which, and the end for which Christ, as King, exercises His dominion, is the Kingdom of God, or the Kingdom of Heaven. His salvation is not applied directly and immediately, nor is His work so individualized that men become its subjects in isolation. Sin was diffused through the activity of one creature of God upon another, and all the sins of men are connected through the organic unity of the race. Grace attains its ends among men in the same way. A thoroughly organized series of agencies has been instituted, for bringing salvation to men. This is implied in the very idea of a Kingdom of God. A Kingdom means not simply power, not simply majesty and glory, but organized power, and majesty, and glory; an adjustment of each member of the Kingdom, and a utilization of all its forces, towards some predetermined end. The smallest hamlet on the most distant border, or amidst the seemingly almost inaccessible recesses of the mountains, and the humblest subject have definitely fixed relations, and are connected by a firm, though invisible bond, to the throne, or head of the administration of His government.

No earthly kingdom has been organized upon a plan so minute and far-reaching, as that of the Kingdom of God. Redemption was in prospect in all God's dispositions for the world that preceded Christ's Coming. Every soul that came into this world, after the Fall, came with reference to the execution of some part connected with the ultimate application of Redemption. The Cross casts its shadow forward in the morning, as well as back ward in the evening of this world's history. Every event of the old world, if it could be read, was a prophecy of Christ's Coming, and a link in the chain, whereby God was bringing to fallen men the riches of His love. Everything was preparatory to the Kingdom of God.

The center of all these preparations was in a nation, to whom God committed the office of proclaiming His promises, and maintaining the hope of the approaching salvation. In order that the idea of the Kingdom of God should be preserved from corruption and be developed from within by conflicts concerning its various earthly relations, that people was kept in isolation. The vision of the future Kingdom was to make its impress, not only upon the lives of individuals, but also upon that of the nation. The worldly spirit in the nation constantly tended towards an externalizing of the Kingdom. Because the Kingdom was to be prepared within Israel, it was identified with Israel itself. The dead shell was substituted for the living kernel. But the very conflict with this externalism developed its inner capacities. The distinction between the inner and the outer sides of the national life, was, until Christ came, only imperfectly understood. With His Coming, the struggle between the true and the false conceptions of the Kingdom was intensified. "The Kingdom of God is at hand," was the cry with which the new order of things began. The entire history preceding the Coming of Christ is only the record of the manner in which the promise was kept alive, and agents prepared for the diffusion of the Kingdom, whenever it would come. Of the greatest character of the Old Testament dispensation, whose closing days were irradiated with the glories of the rising sun, in whose brilliancy he rejoiced that his own feeble light would be lost, it is said that the least in the Kingdom of God would be greater, (Luke 7:28).

With the coming of Christ came the Kingdom. But this was first in great humility and feeble ness. It was like its King, who passed through humiliation, before entering glory. It began within His chosen ones. Its coming was not to them an external matter; but simply an unfolding of what they already had, Luke 17:20-21. It came in power after Christ's Ascension and Sitting at the Right Hand of God. The truth had been taught which was to be the great means for the extension of the Kingdom. The witnesses had been called and had received the revelation into minds whose memory was hereafter to be supernaturally quickened and strengthened. When the Holy Spirit came all things were brought to their remembrance, so that they testified clearly and boldly all that they had seen and heard. Through this testimony the Holy Spirit wrought. By demonstration of the Spirit and of power, it was proved to be not the word of man, but the Word of God. It conquered hearts. It changed the current of lives. It made its enemies its friends and propagators. It made the timid disciples brave. It burst the barriers of the Jewish nation. It claimed to be, and proved, by its ever extending influence, that it was, a Gospel for the world.

Nothing could withstand it. He who sat at the Right Hand of God wielded all the power of Omnipotence to the overthrow of everything that attempted to retard its progress. Was it the Jewish people? Their very opposition became the greatest argument for its truth. Was it the civil government? Within less than three hundred years, it occupied the throne of the Roman Empire. Was it learning? It developed a literature that soon cast into the shade all that had preceded. All that philosophers and poets had previously written that commanded the admiration of men was found to be worthless, except as it contributed to sustain, the religion that had arisen amidst such opposition and detraction. Was it the prejudice of the people? The Gospel of God's Love coming directly in contact with every heart brought to it the message for which it had been yearning, and commended itself to every man's conscience. The powers of nature, and the ingenuity of man, were enslaved to carry it to the ends of the earth. Back of these visible agencies was the activity of the unseen ministers to the heirs of the Kingdom, who turned aside dangers and infused strength and courage whenever they were failing. But a still greater source of power was the presence within them of Jesus Himself. The feeblest witness could say; "I live, yet not I, but Christ, the Almighty King of Heaven and Earth, lives in me. He thinks in my thought, speaks in my word, and lives and acts in everything I do."

The result was not uninterrupted progress and success. The Kingdom was not at once to fill the earth. It was to grow for many centuries amidst constant opposition, unfolding still greater glory with every conflict. It was to grow in individual lives, under the stress of the forces of sin, over which it would triumph, until the struggling ones would be called to the more immediate presence of their Lord. It was to grow in a long line of witnesses upon earth, every trial being only preparatory for ultimate bliss, and every battle being only the signal for an overwhelming victory. The Kingdom of God and the Kingdom of Satan wage a relentless war; but the loss is always Satan's. Even his seeming triumphs are employed to more effectually confound him. With Christ's death, his power was gone, and the weakest believer can successfully oppose him. Man becomes strong as he employs the Word of his King; he is weak as he neglects it. Every period, every crisis, every detail of this great warfare, forms a part of the great plan that has always been a present reality in God's sight. All is comprehended in the statement that, viewed from the standpoint of Redemption, Providence and Grace concur. Providence is occupied with the employment and administration of means for the application of Redemption. "God makes His sun to rise on the evil and the good, and sends rain on the just and on the unjust," Matt. 5:45, because evil and good, just and unjust are alike redeemed, and the blessings of this life are bestowed, in order that, with them, the blessings of everlasting life may be offered.

PART III

THE APPLICATION OF REDEMPTION

CHAPTER XVI
THE DISPENSATION OF THE HOLY SPIRIT

THE Application of Redemption and progress of the Kingdom of God upon earth are dependent upon a special presence of the Holy Spirit, characterizing the period since Pentecost. When it is said, John 7:39: "The Holy Ghost was not yet given; because that Jesus was not glorified," and John 16:7: "If I go not away, the Comforter will not come unto you," there is no denial of the previous presence and activity of the Holy Spirit; it is only another form and degree of His activity that are indicated. David prayed that the Holy Spirit should not be taken from him, Ps. 51:11, and declared that he spoke by inspiration of the Spirit, 1 Sam. 23:2. The prophets of the Old Testament are directly mentioned as writing under the dictation of the Holy Spirit things that they did not understand, 1 Pet. 1:11; they "spoke as they were moved by the Holy Ghost," 1 Pet. 2:21. He had descended upon Christ at His baptism, John 1:32, and all spiritual life that had previously existed had been through His working, John 3:5.

But the presence of the Holy Spirit after Pentecost contrasted with that which preceded, was like the new life that bursts forth on the warm days of Spring, contrasted with that which has struggled and even feebly grown throughout the Winter, or that which luxuriates amidst the tropics, as seen after surveying the stunted vegetation of the Arctic regions. Even those who had enjoyed the public ministry of Christ, and were eye-witnesses of the Ascension as of the Crucifixion, were hesitating and timid until the prophecy was fulfilled: "Ye shall receive power after that the Holy Ghost is come upon you," Acts 1:8; Cf. Luke 24:39. Prior to that, they had been dependent upon the visible presence of Christ; and felt themselves ignorant and helpless when this was removed. They were left alone for a brief season, doubtless, in order that their sense of dependence upon a higher power might be the more deeply realized. Their Master had withdrawn into His invisible glory; and there was no record of what He had said and done, except that contained in their weak memories, confused, as they were, by the multitude of supernatural realities which had been unveiled to them in so brief a time.

The presence of the Holy Spirit had been only sporadic and occasional before Pentecost. At Pentecost, He came to abide forever, John 14:16, with a power, co-extensive with the Gospel that is to be preached to every creature. Under the Old Testament, it had been His office only to impart and nourish the hope of a future salvation in Christ. A vague and indefinite expectancy of Redemption that was in some way to be provided through the Messiah, was the summit which the most devout of that period attained. Their predictions, when read in New Testament light, are found to contain far more than they themselves apprehended. They knew only imperfectly the force of what they spoke and wrote, 1 Pet. 1:11. Even the saints of the Old Testament show more or less of an external relation to the Word of God; their firmest faith and most sincere obedience, are attended with much doubt and hesitation, and with a fear that greatly- checked and impaired their love. The Holy Spirit came at Pentecost, to apply new truths. Under the former dispensation He simply cherished the hope; now He declares and applies the realities of fulfilled salvation. He came at Pentecost, to bring home to every man what was implied in the message of a Savior who had died, risen and ascended to the Right Hand of God for man's sins. He came to assure every man that Christ was now seated on the throne, and was directing all the power of the Universe to bring him where he would reign with Christ eternally. The merely external relation of believers to God's will was over; for He now wrote God's Law on the hearts of men, Heb. 8:10. He made of the general message of the Gospel an individual one, entering into all the details of human history. The new message was no longer confined to a nation, but was now as wide as the race, and as deep as the most remote and obscure experience of every heart.

He came to the disciples, before whom the events of the life of Christ had passed, like the features of a landscape dimly seen as one is hastily carried by it, to enable them to read the record latent in their memories, and to interpret the significance of every act. He came to bring about the effect of a new revelation by recalling to them the words of Christ with infallible accuracy and making these words as they spoke and wrote them, the sources of new divine power. The promise was fulfilled, that from the life of the believer, rivers of living water should flow. "But this He spoke of the Spirit which they that believed on Him were to receive; for the Spirit was not yet given, because Jesus was not yet glorified," John 7:38-39. The office of the Spirit is to testify of Christ, John 15:26, and, with His testimony entering man's heart to create an inner source of life, that is ever to unfold new powers through all eternity, and to issue forth in streams of blessings diffused far and wide. The knowledge of a crucified, risen, ascended and reigning Savior would soon have vanished from the Apostles' minds, and, by its remoteness and exaltation above all that is earthly would have given them no comfort, had it not been forever preserved, refreshed and rendered a matter of constant personal experience by the presence of the Holy Spirit.

For thereby they lived in continuous communion with their unseen and reigning Master. Assured by His witness that they were the sons of God, Rom. 8:17, the facts of the spiritual world and the powers of the Kingdom of God, were to them realities more certain than any to which sense testified, and, as they in turn bore witness, John 16:27, the Holy Spirit wrought through them, Mark 16:20; Acts 1:8. Filled with the Holy Ghost, they spoke as the Spirit gave them utterance, Acts 2:4. With new eyes, they read the Old Testament Scriptures, and, the key to its interpretation now given by the Spirit; they saw in old and familiar words the revelation of what hitherto eye had not seen, or ear heard, or heart conceived, (1 Cor. 2:9-10). Never did the discoverers of what had been long hidden and searched for, proclaim what they had found with greater joy. Aglow with the glories of the new revelation, they could not but speak the things that they had seen and heard, Acts 4:20, even though certain death was the penalty. They spoke not simply as those who had found what the race was yearning to know, but as men divinely-commissioned by their reigning Master to teach all things that He had taught them, and to give to the world, for all time, the witness of their experience. Every creature was to hear it. Through their word the Kingdom of God was to come on earth. Upon the testimony of the Apostles the foundation of the Church was to be laid, and, by the continuance of this testimony the Church was to be built. The Redemption wrought by Christ is applied to men by the Holy Spirit working through the Apostolic Word. For this Apostolic "Word is not the word of man, but of God, "the power of God unto salvation," Rom. 1:16.

CHAPTER XVII
THE WORD

THE Spirit gives no new and immediate revelations. He speaks not of Himself, John 16:13. The Son of God is for all time the sole Revealer. The Spirit is said to reveal only in so far as He recalls what Christ had taught and applies its meaning. He guides into all truth, by receiving from Christ, and declaring what He receives, John 16:15. The entire revelation of God to man to be given in this life, was, therefore, complete, when Christ spoke His parting words to His disciples, as He was taken up into Heaven from Olivet. Men had heard all that was to be heard, and the words, though latent to their consciousness, had been indelibly impressed on their minds. God had spoken once for all through His Son, Heb. 1:2.

This Word was communicated to a few men, in order through them to be communicated to the world. These men were directly divinely called and commissioned to witness, to hear and to proclaim the great facts of the life and death of Christ, the accomplishment of Redemption and the full revelation of God's will that Christ had made. Especially were they to be witnesses of the Resurrection. The truth taught them by Christ and brought to their remembrance by the Holy Spirit, when proclaimed by them, had all the authority and efficacy of what was taught by the voice of Christ Himself. It was not their message, but the message of Christ, so truly, and really, and directly, that He declared: "He that hears you hears Me," (Luke 10:16). The interpretation of the words of Christ by the Holy Spirit, was no less the Word of Christ.

This Word was proclaimed first orally. It was the oral preaching of the Apostles through which the Church was founded. This Word as orally transmitted from generation to generation would have been equally efficacious. As long as an Apostle lived, there was no need that the Word should be otherwise than orally transmitted; for the Apostles were infallible witnesses, and their presence an effectual guarantee against all omissions, suppressions and corruptions.

But the Apostolate, as the office of the divinely-commissioned witnesses of the great facts of Redemption, could not be filled by a succession. New apostles could not be commissioned from those who had not been personally associated with Christ while He walked and spoke among men. The very witness of the Apostles depended upon their having been with Christ from the beginning, John 16:27; and Paul establishes his claim to the office not only by the fact that he had been immediately called, Gal. 1:1, but especially that he had seen Jesus Christ, our Lord, 1 Cor. 9: 1. Hence to all time, there are but twelve Apostles, Rev. 21:14. As persons, the bearers of the office die, but, as Apostles, they remain forever; since they speak to all time through the Apostolic Word received from Christ, and transmitted to the Church.

In order, therefore, to be Apostles not simply to their own generation, but to all nations and ages of the world, they committed their testimony to writing. Through their writings, they communicated to distant lands and centuries not only the contents of their message, but the message itself; not only their thoughts, but their very words. Nothing of the revelation of Jesus Christ is left to the uncertain guardianship of tradition. In all matters of importance in temporal things, we demand that they be made matters of permanent record, that they be committed to writing; so readily may statements concerning relatively unimportant things be perverted and distorted by lapses of human memory, even when there is no motive present for their misrepresentation. But nowhere would corruptions have been so abundant as in matters of divine revelation, not only because they so highly transcend man's comprehension, but especially because of the disturbing element of human sin entering into the life of every reporter, and rendering his record of revelation certainly imperfect, unless protected, as were the Apostles, by the divine endowment of infallibility in what they preached and wrote. Thus the oral and the written Word differ, not in their material—their testimony is one and the same; but only in the form in which this message is clothed. The Holy Scriptures of the New Testament are the infallible record of the Apostolic Word. They are the official presentations of men who, in the exercise of their office as Apostles, or under the direction and authority of the Apostles, could not go astray, as to the words and works of Christ, and to their meaning and application, as developed by the Holy Spirit within the first century, under various circumstances and relations that were to find their repetition in succeeding ages.

Whether, as they wrote, the Word flowed forth in a continual stream from the pen of the sacred writers, and without any effort on their part, or whether each Gospel and Epistle was the result of a process of growth extending through years, in no way affects the divine authority of the New Testament as, in all its parts, the inspired Word of God. As God, by His Providential activity, concurs in every act of man, however insignificant, and directs every item to the working out of a great plan in view from the beginning, so, in the production of any part of His infallible record of revelation, He could just as certainly influence the writer in put ting to writing a narrative concerning the life of Christ, that had grown into a relatively complete form long before, by the frequent repetition of its details in the assemblies of Christians, or in using pre-existing records as the basis of His work, as in directly suggesting every word, while the writer wrote in one continuous and rapid movement. It is enough that we have as the result, whether reached in one way or the other is immaterial, Holy Scriptures of the New Testament that are truly the work of the Holy Spirit, speaking through inspired men; so that not only in every book, but in every verse and word, the twofold testimony of John 15:26-27 is found.

> When the Apostles give their human testimony to Jesus, the Holy Ghost watches over their discourse, guards them from error, purifies, elevates, strengthens their memory, and imparts fitting words; and while each Apostle speaks in his own peculiar way, he is yet wholly imbued with the Spirit. Thus we recognize one

and the same Word to be at the same time both human and divine; appearing as one, we yet acknowledge it to be two joined together, and the god-man's two fold nature in one person is mirrored, as a two-fold, at once divine and human, witness in one and the same Word. All that the Apostles speak is at the same time divine and human.

All that the New Testament claims for the Holy Scriptures of the Old Testament, must be ascribed in an equal, if not a still higher degree, to the Holy Scriptures of the New Testament. The teaching of the New Testament, in such passages as Acts 28:25; 2 Peter 1:21, is most clear and decided to the effect, that the Holy Scriptures of the Old Testament are not a merely human, but a Divine record of Divine revelation. The fuller gift of the Holy Spirit at Pentecost made the human instrumentality only a more complete and perfect medium for the communication of what Christ had taught.

Upon the same principle, the proof of the completion of the record of the Divine revelation in Christ must be determined. None but the Apostles, and those who wrote at their instance or under their guidance, were the official witnesses of what Christ said and did. Only they and those writing under their authority, and with their personal knowledge and supervision, could in any way claim to have that special presence of the Holy Spirit which rendered their testimony infallible. Every book that claims to be a New Testament writing must come with the authority of one who could say: "That which we have seen and heard declare we unto you," 1 John 1:3; "We were eye-witnesses of His Majesty," 2 Peter 1:16; "Have I not seen Jesus Christ?" 1 Cor. 9:1; "I John, saw these things and heard them," Rev. 22:8, viz., the things directly revealed to him by the appearing and words of the Son of God, Rev. 1:1, 17-19.

Through the Word, thus written, the Holy Spirit is ever active. The writing has simply been the guarantee of its purity and permanent preservation. Its efficacy would have been equally as great, if it had never been written; since this depends solely upon its being the Word. The power of God to apply Redemption without the Word is not denied; but we have no promise assuring us of such application. God does not bind Himself, but He binds us to His Word. As we will see, in what follows, every saving operation of divine grace, which is ascribed to the Holy Spirit, is ascribed also to the Word. If Regeneration is ascribed in some passages to the Holy Spirit, in others it is ascribed to the Word; if Sanctification is ascribed to the Holy Spirit, it is ascribed also to the Word. Everything that belongs to the one belongs also to the other. To those perplexed to know the will of God, the Holy Spirit brings the Word, bidding them turn, from all search for His presence in other places and through other means, to the simple Apostolic testimony: "The Word is nigh thee, that is, the Word of faith which we preach," and there is, therefore, no need of searching for Christ in the heights of Heaven or the depths of the abyss, Rom. 10:6-8.

All this Word is found in Holy Scripture. There is no revelation of God, except through Christ, and all God's revelation in Christ is contained in Holy Scripture. There is no Word of God over and beyond or alongside of that contained in Holy Scripture. Even an angel of God who proposes to supplement it, must be rejected as an emissary of Satan, Gal. 1:8. The Word contained in Holy Scripture is not, therefore, only preparatory to a so-called "inner word." Both in the Old Testament and the New, men are turned away from appeals to imaginary supplementary revelations to the simple word contained in Holy Scripture, Isaiah 8:19-20; Luke 16:31. If the Holy Spirit speaks to us, He does so by applying to us some truth contained in Scripture; if the Scriptures are read to or by us, the Holy Spirit is applying His truth through them, and directly addressing us.

It is by the inseparable presence of the Spirit, that the Word of God is "living and efficacious," (Heb. 4:12), and the words of Christ are "spirit and life," (John 6:63). It is this that explains why what is spoken by a few weak and despised men, becomes the means of convulsing the world, of overthrowing deeply-entrenched and firmly-planted error, of successfully opposing seemingly resistless violence, of changing the appearance of the entire fabric of society, of completely revolutionizing human lives. The words of Holy Scripture are efficacious, because they are the words of Him who sits upon the throne of Heaven, and always attends them with His Spirit. His Kingdom on earth advances by the ever progressive appropriation of the truth contained in Holy Scripture by His people. It grows in individuals, as in every perplexity and affliction, they find words of Scripture to direct and console them; and in the Church, as, from age to age, it more fully appropriates the treasures that are there stored up. All true Christian growth, whether it is that of individuals or churches, is a growth in the apprehension and application and assimilation of Scripture. Thus in a certain sense, the Word of God may be said to become incarnate in human lives.

It must, however, be always borne in mind, that the efficacy belongs to the truth conveyed, and not to the words themselves. This truth is just as efficacious, if expressed in other words. More children of God have been converted and been nourished in the divine life by the use of translations, than by that of the original texts of Scripture. The form of the truth has no effect on its efficacy. Wherever the truth is proclaimed, whatever the form is, the Kingdom of God advances. The truth may be conveyed in a confessional statement of a Church, or in a Catechism, or a hymn, or a sermon, or a prayer, or a few sentences that fall in conversation from the lips of a Christian man or woman, or in a religious book. The Holy Spirit pours the material of Scripture into numberless molds, with out in any way diminishing its value. The water of life, drawn into the most worthless earthen vessel, is just as quickening and invigorating, as when it issues immediately from the throne of God. The work of the minister in preaching the Gospel is, from the fullness of his Christian experience, to adapt the material of the Holy Scripture to the peculiar wants of Christian people, as they vary from time to time, and place to place. His sole effort must be in changing the form, in no way to change the material. His ministry is efficacious only as he preaches all the counsel of God, without weakening it by any human admixtures. For it is only the Word of God, through which the Spirit works, and in the use of which he is sure of God's blessing, Isaiah 55:11. All his work as a minister is done, when, like John the Baptist, he bears witness of the Light, John 1:6.

But the truth may be confessed and taught, not only in words, but also in works. A man's life may teach the Word far more extensively or even intensively, than his voice or pen. There are epistles, read of all men, "written not with ink, but with the Spirit of the Living God; not in tables of stone, but in fleshy tables of the heart," 2 Cor. 3:3. The life may either give a general impression of fidelity to Christ, or may stand for the confession of some particular doctrine or duty. Thus the name of Athanasius is forever associated with the doctrine of the Trinity, and of Augustine with the doctrines of sin and grace, and of Luther with that of justification by faith; while those of Schwartz, Ziegenbalg, and Heyer are connected with the duty of evangelizing the world, and those of Howard, and Fliedner, and Florence Nightingale, and Passavant recall various forms of benevolent activity. The martyrs have sealed with their blood their testimony to the truth of Christianity, and the reality of a living communion between Christ and His people on earth. Thus "being dead, they yet speak." A holy personality, i.e., a man or woman sanctified by God's Spirit and living God's Word, diffuses an influence far and wide, and leaves a memory which may refresh and encourage remote generations. A retired Christian mother may thus exert more permanent influence than men whose names are on the tongues of thousands. Christian biography furnishes material for illustrating the Bible beyond all commentaries. A supernatural power attends the confession and living of the truth. The Spirit is just as active in the truth thus taught, as when read or preached. A truly spiritual man attracts to himself spiritually minded men, reproves by his very presence the thought of sin, checks despondency and gloom wherever found, and leads by his own zeal the more feeble onward, where their indifference had hitherto been lingering and hesitating. The same enmity that the world feels towards the Word will necessarily come also to those who stand as the representatives of that Word.

Nevertheless the Word of God in the mouth of a godless man is not inefficacious. Just to the degree that the Word is preached, is the Spirit active. When the Word is preached by the godless, the testimony is conflicting.

Proclaimed in one breath, it is denied with the other, and is not a pure confession of the truth. The life which contradicts the truth causes the effect to be the same, as though a portion of the truth had been withheld. But the promises of God are none the less sure, because a godless man offers them. The commands of God are none the less binding, because a godless man proclaims them. The warnings of God are none the less sure, because a godless man communicates them. Were the efficacy of the Word dependent on the character of the minister, we could rarely be certain that a blessing attends the Word. It is the water of life which brings refreshment, whether received from a golden cup or an earthen bowl.

Nor even does the efficacy of the Word depend upon man's faith. Faith is always necessary to the reception of the efficacy, but not to its presence. There is no lack of efficacy in the medicine which is not taken by the patient. If his symptoms grow worse, he could not tell his physician that there was no efficacy in the prescription. All the while that the wheat was covered by the cerements of the mummy with which it was buried, its efficacy was not lost. Thousands of years elapsed, and when placed in relations favorable to its development, it was proved to have been present. If it had died after a thousand years, and never been placed where it could sprout, this would not have proved any lack of efficacy during that millennium. It is not ground and moisture and sunlight, that give the seed its vitality and efficacy. We find these in an inner principle, which, however, requires for its exercise such external conditions. So the efficacy of the Word depends upon the abiding presence of the Spirit within it, as a life-force, which, however, is not operative in the application of redemption and the salvation of men, unless it secures lodgment in man's heart, and is cherished there. The figure is one which Holy Scripture itself uses in familiar passages.

But in one respect, the figure does not apply. The efficacy of the Word, unlike that of the seed, always has a result. The man to whom the Word of God comes, and who repels it, is not as he was before. Where long and persistently refused, hardening at last comes, Ex. 8:15; 9:12; John 12:40; Heb. 4:1, and the Word becomes "a savor of death unto death," (2 Cor. 2:16). Every word heard or read, every privilege and opportunity enjoyed, leaves its impress either for good or for evil. It is not so properly the Word, as man's abuse of the Word; not so much the efficacy of the Word, as the sin taking occasion of the efficacy that produces this result, Romans 7:8.

CHAPTER XVIII
LAW AND GOSPEL

EVEN when the Word is not repelled, but received, it has a two-fold efficacy, corresponding to the two forms of doctrine which it contains. It proclaims both Law and Gospel. The Law is the declaration of the divine will concerning what man should be, should do and should omit to do. The Gospel is the promise of the gratuitous forgiveness of sins for Christ's sake. All the Law is summed up in the First Commandment, requiring that God should be feared, and loved, and served above all things, and extending its demands over man's entire life and into all its details. Attached to the Law, is its threatening of all its penalties for even the smallest defect in obedience, Gal. 3:10, an offence in but one point being regarded a disobedience of the whole Law, James 2:10, "just as he who steps over one paling gets over the whole fence."

Forcible as are the declarations and demands of the Law in the Old Testament, they acquired a new significance in the New Testament. The Law as taught in the New

Testament, mitigates nothing that is contained in the Old Testament. Christ is not a new lawgiver, offering a new law, which is to give salvation upon easier terms than upon those proposed by Moses. His teaching only showed the demands of the Law had a wider range than had been previously thought. On the one hand, the Ceremonial Law was fulfilled and abolished in Christ; on the other hand, in His repetition of the Law in the Sermon on the Mount, He removed from it the many Rabbinical additions and interpretations with which it had been obscured. But with these external demands abolished, the spirituality of the Law is seen as never before. Judaism had been almost entirely a system of pure externalities. The unity of the Law had been lost sight of. It was disintegrated into numerous isolated precepts, parallel with one another, or which even under circumstances conflicted with one another. All stress was laid upon the outward life, the external duties of morality and the external rites of worship. But Christ taught that the essential thing in keeping the Commandments consisted in the attitude of heart and mind to the Commandments, Matt. 5:22, 28. Keeping the Commandments was not so much a matter of the performance of duties, as it was a matter of love, Matt. 22:37-40. The sum of all duties to God was to love God; the sum of all duties to man was to love man. But the demands of the Law as repeated by Him who came to bring the Gospel, were even more exacting. It was not simply a demand to love God, but to love God with all the heart. It was not simply a demand to love one's neighbor, but by one's neighbor He taught that every man one met was meant, and then the measure of this love was stated as being nothing less than the love of self. All this had been in the Mosaic Law, but had been forgotten, if it had ever been more than superficially apprehended, except by a very few of the more devout in Israel.

In the completeness of Christ's obedience and the sinless perfection of His character, the holiness of the Law was seen in the living example, and the contrast was evoked between it and the sinfulness of men. Nowhere is the wrath of God against sin so forcibly proclaimed as in the sufferings and death of Christ. When the Son of God takes the place of sinful man, the greatness of man's guilt can be seen in the infinite pain inflicted on man's sinless substitute. Sin is shown to be no light and relatively indifferent matter. There is no argument like this, to present the vastness and depths of the Law's demands.

The deeper meaning thus given the Law by Christ's teaching and suffering is pressed upon man in the New Testament by the Holy Spirit. Searching the deep things of Christ, He unfolds more and more of the Law's demands, exalts its standard, and displays God's wrath.

The efficacy of the Law is thus throughout terrifying. It knows of no mercy. Its one word is justice, and since justice has been violated its constant declaration is one of wrath. "Tribulation and anguish upon every soul of man that doeth evil," (Rom. 2:9). It humbles and crushes man, and, unless attained, or followed by the Gospel, drives man to despair. For man's ruin far surpasses all his efforts for self-recovery. "The Law works wrath," (Rom. 4:15), and "by the Law comes the knowledge of sin," (Rom. 3:20).

While the Law and the Gospel must, therefore, be carefully distinguished, as two portions of the one Word of God, they are not contradictory. The one is only preparatory to the other. Everyone who inherits everlasting life does so through the fulfillment of the Law. Unable to fulfill the Law himself, Christ has become to him the end of the Law for righteousness, Rom. 10:4. Law and Gospel concur, the Law being the servant to bring men to Christ, i.e., to lead to the Gospel. All the terrors of the Law have, therefore, beneath them purposes of mercy. They are intended to expel from man all self-confidence, and to lead him to despair utterly of himself, in order that in his helplessness he may be ready to accept Christ, as He comes to him in the Gospel with the assurance of completed Redemption. The Gospel is the entire narrative of what Christ has done and suffered, of what He is and has and will be for sinful men.

> Everything that comforts, that offers the favor and grace of God to transgressors of the Law, is and is properly said to be the Gospel, a good and joyful message, that God does not will to punish sins, but, for Christ's sake to forgive them. (Formula of Concord, p. 593.)

All this is condensed in Melanchthon's admirable definition in the Apology: "The gratuitous promise of the remission of sins for Christ's sake" (p. 115). The effect of the Gospel is, therefore, only peace and joy and life. Assured by it that, even in this life, he has the favor of God, and that God's thoughts towards him are only those of love, all sorrow and sadness are banished from man's heart, except as he recalls his sins, and the voice of the Law is heard condemning them. With the consciousness of God's favor, a new power enters the life and renews it. These effects of the Gospel will be more fully described in what follows concerning the acts of the applying grace of the Holy Spirit.

CHAPTER XIX
WORD AND SACRAMENTS

Thus the Holy Spirit works only through the Word. But the Word of the Gospel comes to man in two different modes. It comes in the testimony of the Apostolic witnesses, recorded in Holy Scripture, and preserved and applied by the Church in that corresponding testimony which, to the end of time, she gives under the impulse and guidance of the Holy Spirit. It comes also through ordinances which Christ instituted, and the Holy Spirit uses, as memorials and seals of completed Redemption, and, by being such memorials and seals, as real means, by which Redemption is applied. These two modes are usually known as the preaching of the Word, and the administration of the Sacraments. Instead of the Word and Sacraments being regarded either as coordinate, or the one as subordinate to the other, they are in fact incapable of comparison or contrast. In the two objects, we have the one Word applied in two different ways. The early Church expressed this by the distinction between the "audible Word," or word, as read and preached, and the "visible Word," or word as applied in the Sacraments.

There is no efficacy or value in a sacrament, except as it is an organ for applying the Word. Luther says of Baptism most forcibly: "If the Word be taken away, the water is the same as that with which the servant cooks;" and he solves the controversy concerning the Lord's Supper, by declaring that his opponents:

> regard the Sacraments as something that we do without the Word of God. There is no Sacrament except as the Word of God is applied to man with an external element. The Word without the element is no more of a Sacrament, than the element without the Word.

The Word comes to the element, and there is a Sacrament. A Sacrament is a divinely-instituted action in which the general promise of the Gospel concerning the gratuitous forgiveness of sins is applied to the individual in the reception of earthly elements, which are offered as pledges of invisible spiritual blessings that are there present and actually conveyed.

The Word outside of and the Word within the Sacrament, are equally precious and efficacious. Nor can any contrast be made concerning different forms of efficacy, as though the Word without an element had a different effect to accomplish within the economy of grace from the Word when joined with the element.

The difference is altogether in the mode in which the Word is applied. As recorded in Holy Scripture and heard in public preaching, it is general, declaring that the mercy of

God is as wide as the sorrow caused by sin, and that the Redemption wrought by Christ is for all men. Even the promises made to the penitent and believing reach individuals, only as through the work of the Holy Spirit, they are led to infer that what belongs to an entire class belongs to every individual of the class, and that what is intended for the human race belongs to every man.

In both of the Sacraments, on the other hand, the Word reaches each individual, not by inference from a general promise, but directly and specifically. Every one baptized has the assurance by the words of promise of Baptism that are applied to him with the water, that God is seeking his salvation, that he is included in the covenant of God's love, and that he can perish eternally only by rejecting God's offers of salvation, and repelling the influences of God's grace. Baptism makes of the general promise of God's grace an individual matter. Every drop of water proclaims that God loves not only the world, but that He loves the particular child baptized, and that to this child every promise recorded in the Gospel most certainly belongs. He need not seek the assurance of his salvation in any secret decree of God; for he has, for all his life, the record in his baptism, that all the blessings of the Kingdom of Heaven have been provided for him, and that they cannot be lost, except by his own rejection and renunciation of this unspeakable gift.

In the Holy Supper, the relation is precisely the same. As the Small Catechism so well declares, the chief things in the Sacrament are the words, that accompany the bodily eating and drinking, viz., the words: "Given and shed for you for the remission of sins." Even the presence of the Body and Blood of Christ is entirely subordinate to these words of the

Lord's Supper. These heavenly gifts only seal the promise of the Gospel.

When I receive the Body and Blood of Christ with the bread and wine, I have in this the most indubitable proof that Christ not only tasted of death for every man, but that His sacrifice pertained to me as truly as though there had been no one else but me who needed redemption. The general promise of the Gospel is individualized with every giving of the bread and every giving of the wine to a communicant; as the words attend it: "Take, eat; this is the Body of Jesus Christ, given for thee. Take and drink; this is the Blood of Jesus Christ, shed for thy sins." Thus there is offered to faith its surest support; since it is the office of faith to change the plural pronouns of the Gospel into the singular number. Instead of saying God loved the world, it says with Paul: "Christ loved me, and gave Himself for me;" and instead of "Christ died for all men," "Christ died for me;" and instead of "our Lord," with Thomas: "My Lord and my God." Christ causes the promise of the Gospel to be offered, not only in *general*, but, through the Sacraments, which He attaches, as the seals of the promise, He seals and thereby especially confirms the certainty of the Gospel promise to every one believing (*unicuique credenti*).

Closely connected with this individualizing or specializing of the Gospel, is the condensation of the Gospel in the Sacrament. The Word as read or preached, presents successively different aspects of the truth. The one truth is divided into its several parts, as the prism resolves the white light into its constituent colors. The Sacraments, however, bring to the individual the condensed Gospel. It is the whole Word of God's grace that is there applied. There is a distinction in the degree of explicitness with which this is done, between Baptism and the Lord's Supper. Baptism contains all that is found in the Lord's Supper, although only in the germ. It is based upon the proclamation of the message of complete redemption, deriving its authority from the direct commission of our Lord, after His satisfaction for sin had been rendered, and, as He was about to ascend to the Father. It is, thus, the seal of the entire manifestation of Christ, bringing the person of the baptized into the full fellowship of all that Christ was, in all His offices and, acts, and words, from His conception by the Holy Ghost, to His sitting at the Right Hand of God.

The Lord's Supper lays its chief emphasis upon the doctrinal presentation of the contents of the Gospel. It is preeminently a memorial of the completion and application of Redemption. The error of Zwinglianism is that it makes it a memorial of the mode, instead of the fact of Redemption. The doctrine of the Real Presence of the Body and Blood of Christ, is what gives the memorial all its force. We need only reflect upon what is comprehended in the assurance that, in the Lord's Supper, the Body and Blood of Christ are actually present with the bread and wine, and are there distributed to all communicants. We need only consider how the Real Presence seals the words that each communicant hears, as he receives the Sacrament. Surely nowhere is the fact of the sin of the communicant and his need of Redemption more forcibly brought to his attention. Beyond the necessity of redemption, it not merely offers the hope that Redemption will be provided; but it declares that such Redemption has been fully made. To remove all doubt, the very Body and Blood, through which Redemption has been effected, are offered. It proclaims the natures of the Redeemer. He is human; for He has body and blood. He is divine; for the

Body and Blood are present and communicated in a mode transcending both sense and reason. None but a body endowed with divine properties could be imparted on the same day to hundreds of thousands of communicants in diverse parts of the world. But above all, it is the pledge of the application of Redemption. No one to whom the words of distribution are applied, if he believes God's assurance, can doubt that Christ died for him, and that the Holy Spirit urges him to accept the benefits of Christ's death. It is not the mystery of the presence of Christ's Body (for the Omnipresence of God, so that all God is at every point of space contains an equal mystery) that has been the obstacle to the reception of the doctrine of the Real Presence among a considerable portion of Protestants; but the main difficulty has arisen from the fact that, in the distribution, in the Lord's Supper, a pastor who holds that Christ died only for the elect cannot say to every communicant: "This is the Body of Christ given for thee." The objective efficacy of the Sacrament is denied, because the objective efficacy of the Word is denied; and the efficacy denied both Word and Sacrament is, according to this theory, found only in man's faith, which is the fruit of God's election. The entire plan of salvation, from its beginning in God's eternal counsel to its consummation in everlasting life, is thus comprehended and declared in the Holy Supper. It is a concentration of the Gospel of Redemption.

The Word, thus individualized and concentrated, is sealed by an earthly element. The element gives weak faith (for perfect faith does not need it) the aid and support of a corporeal contact with the Word. As it is a support to faith for the eyes to see, and the ears to hear some outward visible or audible confirmation of the Word, so with the elements in the Sacrament. The ring assures the bride of the love of her betrothed which has been pledged again and again with his word. The kiss consoles the child who has yearned for a mother's forgiveness far more than do the mere sentences that fall from her lips; but the ring and the kiss without the word would be nothing. Their value lies in that they apply and bear strongest testimony to the value of the word.

The value of the spoken Word lies in its ability to impart a meaning to the mind of the one who hears it. It becomes, therefore, a question that naturally presses for attention, whether the Word, in the Sacraments exercises its efficacy, only when this Word is apprehended by the mind of the recipient. Without doubt, the ultimate end is not reached, until the Word, thus uttered, unfolds its meaning to the intelligence. The Holy Spirit sanctifies, through the truth, as that truth is taught and learned. The efficacy of Baptism is not confined to the moment of its administration; but it continues to follow the baptized person throughout his entire life, as the meaning of the Word, applied in Baptism, and the covenant which God there makes, are more and more unfolded. The remembrance of Baptism is a perennial stream of divine grace, because the Word applied in Baptism was not temporary and transient; but perpetual and eternal. It is not the remembrance of the water that there touched the brow, or the hand of the Church, laid by the minister upon our heads, but of the Word and Covenant of God, that continues to flow, like a stream of living water, throughout our lives. Its abiding testimony is: "For the mountains shall depart, and the hills be removed; but My kindness shall not depart from thee, neither shall the covenant of My peace be removed, says the Lord that hath mercy on thee," Isaiah 54:10. For this reason St. Peter writes to the scattered Christians: "Baptism now save you;" for the influence of the Word that began when the Sacrament was received, continues to work within them, as, by the power of the Holy Spirit, the Word of Baptism is laid to heart, 1 Peter 3:21.

The growth in the apprehension of the meaning of Baptism, as the condition of growth in the appropriation of the blessings of Baptism, implies that in the beginning there was only a feeble apprehension, when contrasted with what was to follow. The analogy of the knowledge of Christ's teaching possessed by the Apostles before the Comforter was given to bring all things to their remembrance, may be recalled. Our constant experience testifies to the influence from the mere presence of men, whose personality leaves an impression upon us, which is expressed only in words when we begin to analyze it. So the presence of the Holy Spirit may influence or produce a temper or disposition of heart and mind, apart from the apprehension of the person influenced, as to the mode in which that effect is produced. If, then, the testimony is clear as to these three things: first, the capacity of children for faith, secondly, their right to Baptism, and, thirdly, Baptism as a means of regeneration, all difficulties connected with their lack of apprehension of what the Word connected with the water means, should not deter us from believing that God has His modes of dealing with them, that are beyond our thought. Faith is a disposition of heart towards God. It is not so much a relation between man and a certain number of truths, as it is a relation of person to person, of man to God, and to the truths, only as, in the truths, God is found. The Holy Spirit may, therefore, as it pleases Him, first work the disposition, or temper, or habit, and afterwards bring the child to the intellectual apprehension of what was there involved. At the time of the Reformation, it was the office of the Lutheran Church to maintain against the Medievalists that faith was properly not an intellectual matter, but was man's trust in God. The influence of divine grace, therefore, begins in the affections and wills of baptized children, upon which the Word of Baptism is to work with their developing intelligence, as they are gradually led into the significance of the truths of which Baptism is the pledge. It would be contrary to the entire tenor of Holy Scripture for us to attribute to Baptism any efficacy, except as it is intended to reach man by changing heart and will. There is no blessing imparted *sine bono motu utentis*. Even in adults, the intellectual side of faith is only preparatory to confidence, as that which really makes faith faith. But that such confidence be wrought, there is no need of first mastering an entire system of dogmatic the ology, or committing the Catechism, or reading the New Testament, or being able to comprehend a sermon. A single sentence may teach all. The Holy Spirit works such confidence through His own appointed means, even before a single sentence may be known or be comprehensible. But when thus wrought, it is only the feeblest germ of that divine life, that is eternally to unfold its capacities, as it progresses in the knowledge of God.

The Holy Supper, however, is only for those who examine themselves, 1 Cor. 11:28. This clearly indicates intellectual maturity, and ability to comprehend the standard according to which the examination is to be made, viz., the Word of both Law and Gospel. A relation between the benefit received and the examination is indicated, since the examination, by its disclosure of sin, leads the communicant to the higher realization of the blessings of the Gospel. We know of no blessing imparted through the Real Presence, except the assurance it gives of completed Redemption. No presence is taught, except in the very moment, when, with the words of distribution, the elements are received. There is no presence taught in Holy Scripture, of the Body and Blood upon the altar, before or after distribution, or in the bodies of communicants, even the fraction of a second after the distribution. The permanent object of the Lord's Supper is the Word of forgiveness. This Word follows the communicant, as the bodily presence is removed, and the Holy Spirit continues to impart through it strength for many days. What God may do farther through the Lord's Supper we know not. It is unsafe to deny absolutely any suggestions that may arise as to the possibilities of His workings. But it is safe to state what Holy Scripture teaches, and on what it is utterly silent; what, if held, comes with divine authority, and what is a matter of purely human conjecture. We know that Christ is bodily present when, through His minister, He says: "Take eat; this is My body;" but we do not know of such presence a moment before or afterward.

There are but two ordinances in which the Gospel promise is thus individualized, concentrated and accompanied by a visible pledge in the use of elements. Circumcision and the Passover in the Old Testament prophesied and foreshadowed the sacraments, but were not such in the proper sense. They pointed to Redemption in the future; but could not proclaim that it was already present. The Absolution in the New Testament so closely approaches the office of a sacrament, that it is not surprising that Melanchthon, in the Apology, designates it as such. Like a sacrament, it individualizes the Gospel promise, but it lacks the divinely appointed element. Confirmation is without divine institution, and is nothing but a very useful and impressive ceremony for admitting members to the full communion of the Church. The Extreme Unction of the New Testament (James 5:14; Mark 6:13) is a different rite from that of more recent times, as its efficacy lay in the prayer, while the anointing was for a medicinal purpose. Ordination contains a blessing, but it has reference to a special grace for the exercise of the duties of the ministry, 1 Tim. 4:14, and is not an ordinance to apply forgiveness of sins. Marriage is not an act, but a relation; and its promises refer not to the spiritual, but to the natural life. Divine institution, though it is, there is no assurance of forgiveness connected with it, there is no proclamation through it of the Plan of Salvation.

As the life of the sacrament is thus the Word of God which it imparts, and the elements are a sub ordinate factor, when the presence of the latter is assured, questions of its mode are of relative unimportance. Such is that of the amount of water to be used and the manner in which it is to be applied, whether by sprinkling, pouring or immersion. Such also are such questions concerning the Lord's Supper, as to whether the bread be of wheat or of rice, leavened or unleavened, broken in or before the distribution, in the form of wafers or not, whether it be given into the hands or into the mouths of the communicants, etc. Nevertheless questions which of themselves are matters of indifference, may, under circumstances, be matters of principle, where the regular order of the Church is arbitrarily set aside or an indifferent matter becomes the badge of error.

CHAPTER XX
THE WORD AND PRAYER

BESIDES the Word and Sacraments, it has been sometimes claimed that Prayer is a means of grace. Nothing can be clearer than the promises concerning Prayer which the Holy Scriptures record, or the encouragements they offer to pray without ceasing, with the firm confidence that the prayer will be undoubtedly answered. God's grace attends and follows every true prayer. When we in everything by prayer and supplication make our requests known unto God, the peace of God, which passes all understanding, keeps our hearts and minds, Phil. 4:6. "You have not, because you ask not," James 4:2. But when, upon the basis of such passages, it is claimed that Prayer is a means of grace, the claim is made from a misconception of what is meant by the expression "Means of

Grace." The Means of Grace are institutions in which God approaches man with the blessings of salvation. Prayer, however, is an approach of man to God. The efficacy of Prayer lies in the Word of God upon which it is based, and which it appropriates. Not every desire of the heart, not every request of the lips, is Prayer. There must be a preceding promise, which faith makes its own, and holds up before God, pleading with Him that it is sure that He cannot be false to His Word, but that this promise will be certainly fulfilled. That only is true Prayer, when there is a fulfillment of what St. John writes: "If we know that He hears us whatsoever we ask, we know that we have the petitions that we desired of Him," 1 John 5:15. Prayer is the voice of faith, and faith comes from and leads to the Word of God.

The Word of God is thus properly the only Means of Grace, whether that Word come to us in its general, or in its individualized form. But in insisting upon the Word as the sole Means of Grace, the error must be avoided that its efficacy is exerted solely by the moral force of the truth it presents. There is a direct influence of the Holy Spirit supernaturally working through Word and Sacrament that gives the truth of Inspiration a power, unlike that which is exerted by all other teaching. It persuades and convicts, not because of the self-evidencing power of the truth, but because it is the organ through which the Holy Spirit reaches hearts. The fact that the Holy Spirit works through means cannot be interpreted as implying that in imparting to the Word efficacy, He Himself is not there. On the contrary, He directs every Word that is spoken, and concurs with it as truly, as though He were immediately acting upon man's heart without any instrumentality.

PART IV
THE EFFECTS OF REDEMPTION

CHAPTER XXI
REGENERATION

THE first end towards which the Holy Spirit works through Word and Sacrament, is Regeneration. Man by nature is spiritually dead. Although he enters this world by birth as a redeemed creature, the first movement of divine grace towards him is to enable him to personally appropriate this Redemption. But for him to do this, in his state of spiritual death, is impossible. He cannot make the feeblest response to the offers of salvation, except through new powers bestowed upon him by the Holy Spirit. The Word might as well be announced to the rocks and mountains, as to the natural man, unless the proclamation of the Word were accompanied by a peculiar and direct energy of the Holy Spirit making man receptive and responsive to the Word. Preparatory, therefore, to Regeneration are Vocation and Illumination. The Call is the bringing of God's Word with its offers of salvation, to men. Illumination is the action of the Holy Spirit accompanying the Call, by which He enables man to understand what is meant by both Law and Gospel. In order that the things of the Spirit of God may be spiritually discerned, the natural darkness of man's mind must be illumined. The knowledge of the letter is important; but it never can be saving knowledge, unless interpreted by the presence of the Holy Spirit. Where grammars and lexicons and philological researches and the opinions of commentators and theologians fail, the Holy Spirit offers a sure interpretation, and makes of it a personal matter for every individual coming under His influence. Such illuminating grace, always attending the Word, may be resisted and checked by man at any stage. Where unchecked, the result is Regeneration. Man is brought to see and acknowledge his sins, to apprehend clearly what is meant in the Gospel, and to appropriate to himself all that is included in both Law and Gospel.

Regeneration, as we first consider it, is the impartation of spiritual life; as generation is the beginning of physical life. It is that act of the Holy Spirit, by which the soul, previously spiritually dead, becomes spiritually alive. But as faith is the organ of our spiritual life, Gal. 2:20, Regeneration must be occupied with the bestowing of faith. It is, on the one hand, the "conferring of the power to believe, *collatio virium credendi*," Quenstedt, John 1:12; and since the restoration of such power is in separable from its exercise, it is the act of the Holy Spirit by which faith is given (*"donatio Jidei*," Hollazius; *salvicae fidei procreatio,* Calovius), Gal. 2:20; 3:26; 1 John 5:1. Thus the Holy Spirit, by one and the same act, gives man the power to believe, and leads him to exercise this power. When Christ said to the man with the withered hand: "Stretch forth thy hand," Luke 6:10, His word carried with it a virtue which enabled the man to do what he had hitherto been unable to do. God, working through His Word, called forth man's act and effectually wrought in it. The hand that had hitherto been dead, became alive, and the forces of life began to move.

Regeneration is not a process, but an instantaneous act of God. When regarded as gradual, it has been confounded either with man's exercise of the new powers therein bestowed, or it has stood for the work of the Holy Spirit whereby faith grows. Regeneration includes only the beginning of spiritual life. The moment the first spark of faith begins, the soul is both regenerated and justified.

Regeneration and Conversion are often con founded. The former refers to the implanting within man of new powers; and the latter to the exercise of these powers in turning from sin. In the former, the Gospel is the instrument; in the latter, both Law and Gospel. Regeneration, in the proper sense, is the work of God alone, in which man's will is absolutely passive. Conversion, when distinguished from Regeneration, is the impulse given the regenerated will by the Holy Spirit, and its consequent activity in turning from sin to God.

Conversion and Repentance are, from the Scriptural standpoint, synonymous. Repentance is often misunderstood, since we read into it the ideas connected with the Latin words, from which it is derived. We think, therefore, of it, as chiefly "sorrow." But, as Luther has so well explained the subject in his letter to Leo X., Repentance is properly "a change of mind" (*metanoia*). It is an act, by which man turns away from what had formerly delighted him to what he had formerly hated. 2 Cor. 5:17 thus applies to both Repentance and Sanctification. He views all things in a different relation, in a new light, and with respect to new ends. Hence Repentance or Conversion has two sides, viz., contrition and faith. Man regards his past life with shame and sorrow; and he looks away from it with joy to Christ, in whom he finds its sins pardoned. As faith grows, so Contrition grows; or using Repentance, in its popular and etymological, although not in its Scriptural sense, the greater the faith, the deeper the Repentance. Contrition is not a matter of the emotions; it is simply man's aversion to sin. The manner in which this aversion affects persons of different temperaments, sexes, ages, and conditions of health must necessarily vary. The different forms of sin in which their guilt has been greatest, also are to be considered. If the aversion to sin be true, the experience of one toward it cannot be made the experience of all. Neither such conversions as those of Paul and Augustine, on the one hand, nor of Timothy and Melanchthon, on the other, dare be made the standard by which to judge those of all Christians.

If theologians be disposed to argue concerning the question concerning what the will of man has to do in Conversion, let them first define what is meant by Conversion. If it means the act whereby man is turned from spiritual death to life, then nothing can more admirably express the true relation of the will, than the very forcible language of the Formula of Concord:

> In spiritual and divine things, the intellect, heart and will of the unregenerate man cannot, in any way, by their own natural powers, understand, believe, accept, think, will, begin, effect, do, work or concur in working anything, but they are entirely dead to good,

and corrupt; so that in man's nature, since the Fall, there is, before Regeneration, not the least spark of spiritual power remaining still present, by which, of himself, he can prepare himself for God's grace, or accept the offered grace, or, for and of himself, be capable of it, or apply or accomodate himself thereto, or, by his own powers, be able of himself, as of himself, to aid, do, work or concur in working anything for his Conversion, either entirely, or in half, or in even the least or most inconsiderable part," (p. 552, §7).

But if Conversion refers to that which occurs in the regenerate, there is undoubtedly a concurrence of man's will, as it has been liberated and quickened and endowed with new powers by the Holy Spirit. The entire controversy is settled by the Catechism, when it says: "I believe that I cannot, by my own reason or strength, believe in Jesus Christ, my Lord, or come to Him."

CHAPTER XXII
FAITH

AS Regeneration consists, therefore, in that act of the Holy Spirit, by which man is given Faith, we come next to the consideration of what is meant by Faith. Whatever may be its meaning elsewhere, it has to do here with a relation of person to person. It is a disposition of man towards God, by which man makes God the center of his life with all its thoughts and activities. God is to Faith the standard of all truth, and holiness, and right, the foundation of all being, the object of every hope and aspiration. Faith is the forsaking of all that is not God or of God, and the seeking for and cleaving to God alone. It is taking God to myself as my all, and commending my all to God, in life, death and eternity. The Faith of Regeneration destroys faith in ourselves and in the world, and leaves alone Faith in God, with all that this Faith comprises. The change designated by Regeneration causes one to give self to Him to whom formerly one had been entirely adverse or hostile.

Faith has its intellectual side; but it is not mere assent to any doctrine or to any number of doctrines. It is essentially a matter of the heart and will. It is the sinking of my will into God's will; the harmonizing of my heart with God's heart. This implies necessarily that all that God reveals, is received without doubt or question, as soon as it is recognized as a revelation of God. The disbelief of revealed truth when that truth is recognized as coming from God, proves the lack of Faith. But revealed truth may be received, as an intellectual matter, and man become a theologian, by correctly stating revealed truth, as he may become a metaphysician, or a scientist, by correctly stating natural truth, without thereby having the Faith which Regeneration gives; and yet the Faith which Regeneration gives requires that everything that is recognized as coining from a Revealing God be believed, as also everything that is recognized as coming from a Commanding God be obeyed. We believe the doctrine, and we obey the commandment, because both doctrine and commandment rest upon the Word of God in whom we believe. Faith is a relation of person to person.

But the very conception of the Word of God as the means of grace, implies that the Holy Spirit offers certain truths for the purpose of communicating through them Faith, and then of strengthening Faith through Faith's continual exercise with these truths. For it must not be forgotten that the truths of revelation have their significance, not as co-ordinate and isolated abstract propositions, but as they constitute an organically-united revelation of God Himself. Everything taught in Holy Scripture is concerning God and His relation to man. Its successive parts only exhibit God to us from various sides. The one truth of God has to be broken into parts adapted to our finite capacities. Our life-communion with God is dependent upon the entrance, into our minds and hearts, of God as revealed from various sides and relations, and upon the attitude of our wills towards this diversified revelation, as its various parts are presented to us.

The center of this Revelation is Christ; since all that God is to us, He is in Christ, and all that we know of God, we know through Christ. Hence, the Faith of Regeneration is concentrated in Faith in Christ. The sum and substance of the Gospel preaching is: "Believe on the Lord Jesus Christ," Acts 16:31. "If you confess with your mouth the Lord Jesus, and believe in your heart, that God hath raised Him from the dead, you will be saved," Rom. 10:9. The center of this center is the doctrine of a dying, risen, ascended and reigning Christ in its relation to my sin and Redemption. Every inspired word of God coming to man in a general form, is accepted by Faith as a personal message; it brings a special and individual blessing to me, from my living and loving Lord.

Faith in Christ implies, therefore, man's conviction that he is a sinner, that by nature he is beneath God's wrath, and that he is helpless, and needs a Savior. It implies the acceptance of Christ, in His divine-human person, and in His various offices and works. It means that I make all that Christ is my own, and give myself over to Christ to be entirely His. It means that I know that He lives in me, and I live in Him; and that there is no relationship in life which is as near and constant, as that between Christ and the soul who accepts His Redemption. We do not mean that Faith enters all at once into the full consciousness of all that is thus implied; but that all these elements are there, and ultimately become the comfort of the believer.

Faith implies more than the probability of the truth of God's promises. It regards them as certainties. Popular usage has diluted the force of the expression: "I believe," until it has often become little more than: "I guess." This has arisen from the perversion of the meaning of Faith in Christ. On the contrary the Epistle to the Hebrews declares Faith "the substance of things hoped for, the evidence of things not seen," Heb, 11:1. St. Paul explains: "I know whom I have believed, and am persuaded that He is able to keep that which I have committed unto Him," 2 Tim. 1:12. St. John exhorts: "I have written unto you, that you may know that you have eternal life," 1 John 5:13. St. Paul warns that doubts concerning the absolute certainty of the application of God's promises to believers, endanger their salvation, in the words: "Know ye not your own selves, how that Jesus Christ is in you, except ye be reprobates?" 2 Cor. 13:5. All that is less than absolute certainty is doubt. Doubt is disbelief. It is the regarding that, as possibly false, which God has declared to be true, i. e., making God a liar. Nevertheless such is the weakness of man, even when the work of grace has begun in him, that Faith has constantly to struggle with doubts, and the prayer to be constantly on the lips: "Lord, I believe, help Thou mine unbelief," Mark 9:24. But just in so far as there is lack of complete certainty, Faith is imperfect and sinful. The model presented us in Scripture is that of Abraham, "who, against hope, believed in hope, being persuaded that what God had promised, He was able also to perform," Rom. 5:18, 21.

The certainty of Faith is not a human persuasion, arising from any process of reasoning upon the basis of the evidences of the truth of Scripture, or from the effects of Faith in the life. It is the work of the Holy Spirit, testifying in man's heart to the truth, "the Spirit bearing witness with our spirits that we are the children of God," Rom. 8:16, "the anointing," teaching believers of all things, 1 John 2:27, the sealing of believers "with that Holy Spirit of promise," Eph. 1:13.

Faith not only has its degrees, but it also has its perils. Faith may be lost. The restored spiritual life may depart. We cannot interpret the constant warnings of the New Testament to believers in any other way. The falls of David and Peter would be inexplicable, were it otherwise. The testimony is explicit to the fact that, while, in some cases, where Faith has been lost it has been restored, and that the Holy Spirit follows the erring one as David and Peter were followed, in order to lead them to repentance, in other cases the departure has been permanent, Heb. 6:4-6. We cannot enter here into the treatment of the Sin against the Holy Ghost, except to call to mind the fact that no one has committed this sin, with whom the Holy Spirit, still strives, and in whom there is the least anxiety concerning the sin. Such anxiety indicates that the person has not been absolutely deserted by the Spirit, and that the grace of God is still endeavoring to win him back to the high estate whence he has fallen. The same Lord who bade Peter forgive his brother, if he were to transgress against him and return seventy times seven times, Matt. 18:22, will not do less towards those who return to the covenant of God's grace. If there are those who have been regenerated, who ultimately perish, the reason is not only that they fell from God's grace, but especially because, after falling, they would not return. As the Apostle describes his anxiety in bringing back the Galatians to the grace whence they had fallen, in the words: "My little children, of whom I travail in birth again until Christ be found in you," Gal. 4:19, so the

Lord Himself tells the secret of man's ruin from first to last, when He declares: "I would, but ye would not," Matt. 24:37. It is man's continued hostile attitude towards the means, by which the Holy Spirit works Faith, that prevents his salvation, whether he has, or he has never been regenerated. God does not recall His promises, or with draw His grace; but man casts himself outside the sphere within which grace works. God's side of the covenant is permanent. When it is broken, it is broken by man; and when it is restored, it is restored through the reclaiming efforts of the Holy Spirit in influencing man's return to its terms. "If we believe not, yet He abideth faithful, He cannot deny Himself." Man who has fallen may read in his baptism, God's disposition towards him, which remains unaltered, except, as man is indifferent to the blessings there provided, and the promises there announced.

Nowhere is this taught more forcibly than by Luther in his Large Catechism:

> Our baptism abides forever; and even though some one should fall from it and sin, we nevertheless always have access thereto, that we may again subdue the old man. Repentance is nothing else than a return and approach to baptism, that we return to and practice what had been begun and had been abandoned. I say this in order that we may not fall into the opinion that our baptism is something past, which we can no longer use, after we have fallen again into sin. The reason is that it was regarded only according to the external act, once performed, and completed. This arose from the fact that St. Jerome wrote that "repentance is the second plank, upon which we must

swim forth and cross over after the ship is broken." This expression is not correct, or else never rightly understood. For the ship never breaks, because it is the institution of God, and not a matter of ours; but it happens that we slip and fall out of the ship. Yet if any one fall out, let him see that he again swim up and cling to it.

Nor is Calvin lacking in a similar testimonial to the permanent efficacy of God's promise as applied in baptism:

> Though all men were false and perfidious, yet God ceases not to be true; though all men were lost, yet Christ remains a Savior. We confess, therefore, that during that time we received no advantage whatever from baptism, because we totally neglected the promise offered us in it, without which baptism is nothing. Now since, by the grace of God, we have begun to repent, we accuse our blindness and hardness of heart for our long ingratitude to His great goodness; yet we believe that the promise itself never expired, but, on the contrary, we reason in the following manner: By baptism, God promises remission of sins, and will certainly fulfill the promise to all believers; that promise was offered to us in baptism; let us, therefore, embrace it by faith: it was long dormant by reason of our unbelief; now let us receive it by faith.

CHAPTER XXIII
FAITH OF INFANTS

THE question whether infants can be regenerated is the same as whether infants can have faith. If everything that characterizes the faith of adults be regarded essential to faith, i.e., if faith, at an advanced stage of development be made the universal test of faith, we cannot ascribe it to infants. The Scholastics laid great emphasis on the intellectual side of faith. "To believe," says Thomas Aquinas, "implies the consideration of the intellect, combined with examination and consent on the part of the will." "To believe is an act of the intellect assenting to divine truth, arising from a determination of the will impelled by grace." This means that faith can exist only as a truth is presented to the intellect, to which after deliberation, inquiry and examination, the will determines to assent. The Reformers were especially emphatic in maintaining that this conception overlooked the most important element of faith, viz., confidence. The dogmaticians accordingly added "confidence," and analyzed the entire conception of faith into the three elements of knowledge, assent and confidence. But since where there is no confidence there is no faith, knowledge and assent do not belong to the essence of faith. They are the pre-requisites of a mature faith. They are inevitably found where there is faith in a doctrine. I cannot, in the proper sense, believe a doctrine unless I have been taught what it is, and assent to it, and then determine that my life shall be regulated according to it. Such faith in the doctrines of revelation will be the necessary result of faith in the person who reveals them. But the essence of faith given in regeneration, is confidence or trust in a person. It is that temper or disposition of the heart towards God by which the person is rendered capable of receiving whatever God offers, and of responding to every word of God, through new powers wherewith God has endowed him.

Infants are, therefore, incapable of acts of Faith, although they have a habit of Faith; just as they are incapable of acts of sin, although they have, in natural depravity or Original Sin, a sinful habit. We say that men have an innate knowledge of God. By this we do not mean that they are conscious of the existence and presence of God, and of any relations in which they stand to Him; but only that the human mind is endowed with faculties that inevitably draw the conclusion of the existence and of certain attributes of God from the contemplation of Nature. In like manner, we claim that when, on the basis of certain texts of Scripture, we teach the possibility of infant regeneration, the faith that is therein said to be wrought, must correspond to other determinations of their spiritual nature. The Faith of infants is like the knowledge and the sin of infants. The actual presence is not disproved by the fact that it is not consciously present. The Faith may lie dormant, like the words of Christ to the Apostles, until the Holy Spirit recalled them, or like the attainments of a scholar while he is sleeping.

We may again quote Calvin, because he is often regarded as the representative of a school most remote from such doctrine. The possibility of the regeneration of infants, he finds to be a necessary member in the argument for Infant Baptism. Answering the objection to Infant Baptism that infants cannot be regenerated or believe, he says:

> Their objection, that the Holy Spirit, in the Scriptures, acknowledges no regeneration, except from "the incorruptible seed," that is, "the Word of God," is a misinterpretation of that passage of Peter, which merely comprehends believers who had been taught by the preaching of the Gospel. To such persons, indeed, we grant that the Word of the Lord is the only seed of spiritual regeneration; but we deny that it ought to be concluded from this, that infants cannot be regenerated by the power of God, which is as easy to Him, as it is wonderful and mysterious to us. Besides, it would not be safe to affirm that the Lord cannot reveal Himself in any way so as to make Himself known to them.
>
> But our opponents say "Faith comes by hearing," of which they have not yet acquired the use, and they cannot be capable of knowing God; for Moses declares them to "have no knowledge between good and evil." But they do not consider, that when the Apostle makes hearing the source of Faith, he only describes the ordinary economy and dispensation

of the Lord, which he generally observes in the calling of His people. I would beg them to inform me, what danger can result from affirming that they already receive some portion of that grace, of which they will ere long enjoy the full abundance. For if the plenitude of life consists in the perfect knowledge of God,— when some of them, whom death removes from the present state in their earliest infancy, pass into eternal life, they are certainly admitted to the immediate contemplation of the presence of God. As the Lord, therefore, will illuminate them with the full splendor of His countenance in heaven, why may He not also, if such be His pleasure, irradiate them with some faint rays of it in the present life; especially if He does not deliver them from all ignorance before He liberates them from the prison of the body? Not that I would hastily affirm them to be endued with the same Faith which we experience in ourselves, or at all to possess a similar knowledge of Faith, which I would prefer leaving in suspense; my design is only to check their foolish arrogance, who presumptuously assert or deny whatever they please.

But far more important than the testimony of theologians is that of Holy Scripture. It declares absolutely that without Regeneration, there is no entrance into the Kingdom of God, John 3:3-5, and, just as clearly and plainly, that the Kingdom of God is for infants as well as for adults, Matt. 19:14; Luke 18:16. Christ Himself expressly declares that there have been little children who believed in Him, Matt. 18:6; Mark 9:42. As infants as well as adults are comprehended in Redemption, the Holy Spirit has His own way of applying to them

Redemption and bringing them to Faith. The Faith of infants is that disposition towards God which is effected by the application of Redemption. In John the Baptist, this disposition was imparted without the use of means, and even before birth, Luke 1:15. If God, therefore, impart Regeneration without means, as we believe He does also in infants who die unbaptized, what should prevent Him from accomplishing the same ordinarily through Baptism, His appointed means for that purpose, John 3:5; Tit. 3:5; Eph. 5:26; Gal. 3:27; 1 Pet. 3:21? He does not reach them through the Word, as heard or read. Nor does He reach them through the Lord's Supper. The only means of grace that is left is Baptism.

CHAPTER XXIV
JUSTIFICATION

INSEPERABLE from Regeneration is Justification. Everyone living in the grace of Regeneration is justified. Every justified person is regenerate. The end of Regeneration is Justification, as it is the office of Regeneration to impart faith, and, through faith, there is Justification. But the necessity of drawing a sharp distinction becomes manifest, when it is remembered that Regeneration is a work of the Holy Spirit within man, while Justification is a change of relation between God and man, and is, therefore entirely external. Man is not justified by the work of the Holy Spirit whereby faith is wrought. His Justification is found entirely in that which is outside of and beyond Himself, viz. , in that all-sufficient righteousness, provided for him in the work and sufferings of Christ, the God-man, during the thirty-three years of His visible stay on this earth, over eighteen hundred years ago. Regeneration simply furnishes man with the means whereby he appropriates to himself this righteousness. The three chief acts of the applying grace of the Holy Spirit may be distinguished thus:

Regeneration:
An act
God alone
Internal
Instantaneous
Equal
Perfect
From death
Gives faith
Quickens man

Justification
An act
God alone
External
Instantaneous; constantly repeated
Equal
Perfect
From guilt
Pardon and title to heaven
Reconciles God

Sanctification
A process
God and man
Internal-External
Gradual
Unequal
Partial in this life
From defilement
Holiness
Restores God's image

To appreciate the nature of Justification we must review all that has been said concerning the work of Christ. Justification is the application of that work in the strictest sense. By Justification, all that Christ has suffered and done actually becomes the property of the individual believer. It has been his by right before; now it becomes his by actual possession. In Christ, God looks with favor upon the entire human race; outside of Christ, He looks with favor upon none of our race. In Christ, He has actually forgiven all men; out of Christ, He has forgiven none. Justification is, therefore, that act by which God, finding an individual in Christ, accounts, as though they were his, all that Christ has done and suffered. The one thus regarded, is made, in God's account, the righteous one that Christ was, during the years in which He was subject to the Law, and bore the burden of our sins. Every charge against Him is cancelled. Every shame is covered. Every spark of anger in God's heart is quenched by the Blood of Christ. God has towards him no other thoughts but those of love. His love for him is just as ardent as His anger was consuming. He, who is justified, is far more than a forgiven sinner. He has been furnished with the full and complete title to all the rewards which Christ's obedience to the law has earned. There is absolutely nothing more for him to fear except his own weakness. There is nothing for him to expect but ever new realizations of the blessedness that, with Christ, he has received.

That this is the meaning of Justification is clear from the entire teaching of Holy Scripture. The proof is not dependent upon a few pages scattered here and there, and torn from their connection, but it underlies the entire revelation of the Gospel. That the word "justify," outside of this article, may sometimes mean to make one inherently righteous is not denied. Nor is it denied that Justification, as an act of the applying grace of God, is always attended with incipient righteousness, and that the justified man at once begins to be a holy man. The question here has to do exclusively with the ground upon which sinful man is forgiven and declared worthy of everlasting life. This is entirely what Christ is to him, and not what he is in Christ.

The argument may be briefly recapitulated as follows:
1. The word "to justify" was habitually used among the Hebrews to indicate the legal vindication of a person before a court of justice. Deut. 25:1; Ps. 82:3 ("do justice," literally "justify." Cf. 2 Sam. 15:4; Is. 43:9.

2. This is still more manifest by the fact that "to justify" and "to condemn" are sometimes contrasted. Prov. 17:15; Deut. 25:1; Is. 50:8; Matt. 12:37; Rom. 8:33-34; 5:16.

3. "Justify" is thus used in a forensic sense, without regard to the question whether the cause is righteous or unrighteous. Is. 5:23; Prov. 17:15.

4. From a human, it is transferred to God's tribunal, where "to justify" carries with it also the meaning of conferring the rewards that are due the righteous and innocent. Ex. 23:7; 1 Kings 8:31-33.

5. It acquires also the general meaning of "to approve, or acknowledge as righteous." Luke 7:29, 35; 16:15; 10:29; Matt. 11:19.

All these items pertain to the proof that the word has such meaning even in other relations than that of the justification of the sinner before God. But that it has this meaning here, is the great theme of the Gospel, as St. Paul has so clearly shown, especially in the Epistles to the Romans and the Galatians. Read only the third chapter of Romans, and follow the argument. The Law, it says, shows that all are under sin, stopping every mouth and condemning all as guilty before God, because, by its deeds, no flesh can be justified. But we are justified freely, i.e., without the deeds of the law, Romans 3:19-20, 24, 28. In Romans 5:16, the judgment of the Law to condemnation is contrasted with the free gift, which notwithstanding man's many offences is justification. The transfer from Romans 7 to Romans 8 contrasts the way of Salvation by the Law, with that through the Gospel, and shows that Justification is found only in the latter, Rom. 8:2-3. "Justifying" according to Rom. 8:33 is the not laying of anything to the charge of God's elect; it is not condemning, Rom. 8:34. According to Rom. 10:3, it is the not having one's own righteousness, but having the righteousness of Christ. Even though man were unconscious of any sin, he could not find in this his justification, 1 Cor. 4:3-4, because he is here judged not in man's judgment, but in that of God.

But God does not justify without a ground of Justification. The guilt and punishment of man's sin are not annihilated. Every penalty of transgression is exacted. All the disgrace of sin must have someone to whom it is imputed. God does not declare man righteous and worthy of everlasting life, unless there is actually presented a complete equivalent for the most far-reaching demands of the Law. God's mercy is not exercised at the expense of His justice. But, in Justification, the righteousness of Christ is accounted ours. Christ stands before God charged with our sins; and we stand before God, with all Christ's merits, regarded as ours.

It is not, then, our life in Christ, or Christ's life in us that justifies us, but it is alone what Christ was for us, when He was made sin for us who knew no sin, that we might be made the righteousness of God in Him, 2 Cor. 5:21, when He bore our sins in His own Body on the tree, that we, being dead to sins, should live unto righteousness, 2 Peter 2:24. It is not what Christ is for us now, or what He will be to us in Eternity, or what He has been for us during the period since His Resurrection and Ascension, but entirely what He was for us during the thirty-three years of Humiliation that is the ground of our Justification. This has been explained already under Redemption.

The righteousness of Christ, provided and offered to all, is individually appropriated by faith. What grace has already made ours by right, through faith becomes ours by possession and full use. This faith is given man in Regeneration. It justifies, not because it is the root of a holy life, not because God accepts it as an equivalent for a holy life, nor even because through it Christ dwells in us, and the Holy Ghost is given, and man becomes a temple of God. But we are justified by faith, Romans 5:1, because God has made faith the instrument whereby we take to ourselves and use against all the accusations of the Law, and offer, in answer to all the promises of eternal life, all that has been provided for us in Redemption. By faith all the rewards of Christ's State of Humiliation are made mine.

We are not only justified by faith; but we are justified by faith alone. Faith is never alone; because wherever there is faith, there is the Holy Spirit, and the Holy Spirit is always active. But the new life, thus quickened, has nothing to do with Justification, except as it is the inevitable result of Justification. Probably the relation cannot be better stated than this: Wherever there is faith, there is love and a holy life, because wherever there is faith, there is Justification, and wherever there is Justification a holy life immediately begins. If the new life that accompanies and follows faith were made a concurrent instrument in Justification, the ground of

Justification would no longer be the merits of Christ alone, but it would be partly the merits of Christ, and partly our own holiness. We are justified by faith alone without works, because our Justification is found entirely in Christ, and we accept Christ, not by works, or love, or a holy life, but entirely -and alone by faith- We may well regard the entire situation, as though there were neither love, nor any gift of the Spirit within us—not even faith—and we could only turn away from ourselves, overwhelmed with the sense of our spiritual poverty, and point to the Cross with the words: "There is all my righteousness." Thus the efficacy of faith lies entirely in the object which it apprehends. There is no virtue in faith of itself. Faith apprehending anything but a promise of God is worthless. Faith apprehending God as Creator, or as Sanctifier, does not justify. Nor does faith in our faith, or in our assurance of faith justify. Men are justified solely by faith in God as Redeemer. We are justified solely by the merits of Christ apprehended by faith, or, otherwise stated, by faith apprehending the merits of Christ. This alone makes the righteousness of Christ ours.

This faith is not, as sometimes misrepresented, simply a belief in a doctrinal proposition, as though we are justified by faith when we believe that we are justified by faith. It is confidence in a person. It is man's complete submission in intellect, affections and will to Christ. It is man's finding in himself nothing that is good, and holy, and right, and his finding his all in Christ. He is justified by faith alone when, recognizing his utter ruin by nature, he gives himself to Christ, as his wisdom and righteousness, his sanctification and redemption.

Justification has no degrees. There is no such a thing as a partial Justification. Man is either completely forgiven all his sins, or he is forgiven none whatever. The ground of Justification being always Christ's merits, either all of His merits are ours, or none are ours. Even the weakest faith makes us partakers of Christ's righteousness; and hence the weakest faith justifies as fully as the strongest faith, since it is not properly faith, but the object that faith apprehends, that justifies.

Justification is therefore instantaneous. The very moment that the feeblest faith in Christ as a Redeemer is enkindled, man is justified. But while instantaneous, it is an act of God, that is constantly repeated. Man's nature, until the end of life being infected with sin, needs, when regarded by itself, constant forgiveness. Hence, even the justified, as they survey themselves, daily turn to God, with the prayer: "Forgive us our trespasses." Assured that they are forgiven, they crave continually renewed forgiveness; for the inner corruption is ever making itself felt in fresh offences. This is the daily sorrow and repentance for sin, of which Luther wrote in the first of his Ninety-five Theses, in which he said that "when our Lord Jesus said: 'Repent,' He meant that the entire life of believers should be a repentance."

It is the person, and not the sins that are forgiven. When the sins are said to be forgiven, the meaning is that the person is forgiven his sins. It is, impossible, therefore, not only for some sins to be forgiven, while others are unforgiven, but also for the guilt of sin to be forgiven, while its punishments or some of its punishments remain. For "there is, therefore, now no condemnation to them which are in Christ Jesus," Rom. 8:1. To those who have the righteousness of Christ, there belong only the full and complete rewards of that righteous ness. God is never angry with His justified child. He has for it no thought except those of pure and complete love. The reconciliation is perfect. Man has courage to feel at home with God, and to address Him, not from a distance, and in the language of constrained and reverential awe, but with even more freedom than the most affectionate child approaches the best and tenderest of parents. He is nearer and dearer to God, and God is nearer and dearer to him, than mother and child are to one another.

CHAPTER XXV
SANCTIFICATION

JUST as inseparable as Justification is from Regeneration, is Sanctification from both. The transformation of character known as Sanctification or Renovation begins immediately with Justification. The very presence of faith sanctifies; for the presence of faith means the presence of the Holy Spirit, the Sanctifier. It means the presence of Christ in the believer, as St. Paul declares that he lives, yet not he, but Christ in him, Gal. 2:20. Faith at once enkindles love. We cannot believe in Christ without loving Him. "We love Him; because He first loved us, " 1 John 4 : 19. The more the love of Christ towards man is contemplated, the deeper grows man's love, Rom. 5:8. As the love of Christ is regarded, not simply externally, but, as a matter of the believer's Christian experience, in his daily and hourly communion with Christ, his love to Christ is ever growing. Through this love, faith works, Gal. 5:6. "The love of Christ constraineth us...that they which live should not henceforth live unto themselves, but unto Him which died for them and rose again," 2 Cor. 5:14-15.

The passage in Luther's Introduction to the Epistle to the Romans, in which he describes the energy and activity of faith, is classical and deserves to be inscribed in letters of gold upon every memory:

> Faith is not man's opinion and dream...but it is a divine work in us, that changes and begets us anew of God, John 1:13. It mortifies the old Adam, transforms us into entirely different men in heart, mind, will, sense and powers, and brings with it the Holy Ghost. Oh, this faith is a living, busy, active, efficacious thing, so that it is impossible for it not incessantly to do good works. It does not ask whether good works are to be done; but before the question has been asked, it has already done them, and is always doing them. But he who does not these works, is a faithless man, who is always groping and looking for faith and good works; and nevertheless knows neither what faith or good works are, though he prate in many words concerning faith and good works.

A similar description, Luther has given in his Commentary on Genesis:

> Faith is a change and renewal of the entire nature, so that ears, eyes and heart hear, see, feel and think entirely differently from other men. For faith is a living and powerful thing; it is not an idle thought, neither does it swim upon the heart, like a fowl upon

water. But as water, warmed by fire, while remaining water, nevertheless is no longer cold, but is warm and an altogether different water, so faith, as a work of the Holy Ghost, forms another mind and other senses, and makes man entirely new. Faith, therefore, is a toilsome, difficult and powerful thing.

The work thus beginning inwardly by the presence of the Holy Spirit in the heart, the external side of Sanctification is to be regarded, only as it is a true expression of what has been inwardly experienced. The tree must be made good before the fruit can be good, Matt. 12:33. When hearts are purified by faith, Acts 15:9, everything proceeding from them is holy. The Holy Spirit diffuses His influence through the sanctified personality of the believer. The believer is a new creature in Christ Jesus, in whom all things have become new. His disposition towards God, his views of truth, his standard of judgment, his objects of admiration, his motives, his hopes, his entire life are new. Instead of seeking only self, he seeks for God; instead of living only for earth and time, he lives for Heaven and eternity; instead of clinging only to what he can see and feel, he clings to what is beyond the range of sight and sense. His character deepens as the eternal and unseen more and more predominate in all that he thinks and does. The Holy Spirit works through him; and he cooperates with the Holy Spirit in the exercise of the new powers with which he is endowed. All that he is and has is directed towards this end. With heart intent upon God's will, he loves all that God wills and, so far as he is sanctified, does all that God directs. He is "created in Christ Jesus unto good works, which God hath before ordained that we should walk in them," Eph. 2:10. He glorifies God by a holy life. The importance of

Sanctification is in no way diminished by the fact that we cannot find our Justification in it, or, that only those who have been first justified can enter upon a sanctified life.

Unlike Justification, Sanctification is gradual, and has its degrees. The old man is more and more put off, and the new man more and more put on. "Though our outward man perish, yet the inward man is renewed day by day," 2 Cor. 4:16. The power of grace more and more subdues the remnants of natural depravity, which constantly tempt to sin. Through this struggle, the child of God constantly advances towards perfection. He works out his salvation, while God works in him, Phil. 2:12-13.

But with all his efforts, until the close of life, he cannot reach perfection. No one, except the Son of God, has ever lived on earth, who could not pray the Lord's Prayer, with its petition for forgiveness, at the conclusion of every day's work. The experience of the Apostle Paul, as described in the Seventh Chapter of Romans, is that of every Christian. The struggle is never over, until, at death, the sinful flesh is entirely laid aside. The daily repentance of the Christian testifies to the imperfection of the renewal, even when it is best. The express words of St. John concerning the terrible self-deception, into which those fall who profess to be without sin, ought to be sufficient, 1 John 1:10. The passages by which an attempt is made to teach the possibility of sinless perfection in this life, are, either such as set forth the demands of the Law, which is never satisfied with less than perfect obedience, and constantly reveal man's imperfection, Matt. 5:48; or such as are relative, as 1 John 4:12, where it is taught that the measure of love is the measure of perfection, and 1 John 3:9, where the meaning is that, so far as the new life, imparted in Regeneration, controls man, he cannot sin;

or such as teach the perfection of the righteousness which becomes the believers in Justification, not in Sanctification, Gal. 5:16, etc. The difference between the believer and the unbeliever is that, while, in the former, sin is ever present, Rom. 7:21, sin no longer reigns, Rom. 6:21, as in the latter, but is constantly losing ground.

CHAPTER XXVI
GOOD WORKS

THE progress of Sanctification is marked by good works, and the new life is exercised in good works. A good work is a fruit of faith in act, whether that act is within the heart, or in the outward life. It is a free act of a justified person, which he performs out of love to God. It has both its source and its standard in the Word of God. Faith acts not upon its own impulse, but as it has received a word of God. Hence good works are no self-chosen acts of self-denial or heroism, but they are simply the fulfilling of the Ten Commandments. In these Commandments, there is comprised for all time the full sum of man's duty. They are repeated and expanded and expounded by our Lord in the Sermon on the Mount, whose aim is particularly to present the spiritual side of the Commandments. He also sums up the permanent elements of the Ten Commandments, of which not a jot or a tittle shall pass until all is fulfilled, Matt. 5:18, in such summaries as Matt. 19:18, 19; 22:37-39. The perfection towards which man is to strive, consists in fulfilling all these. There is nothing more that he can do. There are no so-called "evangelical counsels," whereby man can do more than his duty, and acquire merit by so-called "works of superogation." When he has done all, he has done no more than his duty, and is an unprofitable servant, Luke 17:10. Man cannot, therefore, bind himself by a vow to perform what was not incumbent upon him before. The vows of poverty, chastity and obedience are commendable only if they express duties incumbent upon the person without the vows, but which he fully acknowledges through the vows. All the works of the Ten Commandments are, therefore, holy; because they cannot be wrought without the Holy Spirit, and, because through them all, God is glorified. The ordinary are no less holy than the extraordinary duties. The most menial offices of the humblest men are equally holy with those which are occupied with the peculiar exercises of religion. The "religious life" of the great mass of Christian people necessarily becomes chiefly that of providing for and attending to very insignificant things, the details of a trade, the cares of a family, the toil and worry of housekeeping, obedience to a master or magistrate. To disparage or forsake these works for others of imagined superior holiness, not included in God's Commandments, is to forsake the path of good works. This must be constantly brought into prominence, against the assumptions of monastic holiness, as well as against tendencies prevalent in what seems the most opposite extreme within Protestantism.

There is probably no place where the treatment of doctrine has to be more carefully guarded, than in enforcing the duty of good works. That it is a most important part of the preaching of the Christian minister is manifest from Tit. 3:8: "I will that thou affirm constantly that they, which have believed in God, might be careful to maintain good works." The danger lies in so enforcing this duty, that the doctrine of Justification by faith alone is obscured. This danger is avoided, when it is clearly taught that the necessity for good works, arises not from the necessity for salvation, since neither salvation, nor continuance in a state leading to salvation depends upon man's good works, but from the fact, that it belongs to the nature of the Christian to perform good works, just as it belongs to the nature of the sun to shine, or of fire to burn. So far as the processes of grace have pervaded his nature, he is thankful for every opportunity of becoming a co-worker with God, just as an affectionate child cannot aid soon enough in the occupations of his parents, and even the plays of childhood foreshadow coming duties. The Law is declared to the child of God, as the will of that Father, in doing whose will he finds his chief delight. "Ours teach that it is necessary to do good works, not that we may trust, that we deserve grace by them, but because it is the will of God that we should do them" (Augsburg Confession, Art. XX). Nothing that God has commanded will be regarded by His child as unnecessary. Nor will anything be so regarded, in which he has the assurance that God delights. The debt of gratitude which he owes God, for his creation and redemption, his regeneration and justification, will ever find in good works acknowledgment and expression. He recognizes in good works a part of the chain of instrumentalities, whereby God is conducting him towards the ultimate attainment of the full fruits of Redemption. For the end of Redemption was not only Justification, but also that "He might purify unto Himself a peculiar people, zealous of good works," Tit. 2:14. Indifference concerning them must be regarded as indicating either the entire absence of faith, or the presence of a spiritual disease weakening faith, and threatening the near approach of spiritual death.

Nevertheless, even at best, since Sanctification is in this life incomplete, there are no absolutely good works. The best works of the best men are stained by sin. No one can point to any single act of obedience and exclaim: "That at least was rendered with absolute perfection." We must pray for the forgiveness of even our best efforts. So far as works are good, they are such because of the presence and activity, within man, of the Holy Spirit. Hence they are called the fruits of the Spirit, Gal. 5:22, 23, and only as such are pleasing to God. How little merit can they have for man, when all of them that is good, comes from the Holy Spirit!

But while good works have no merit, they have their rewards. In maintaining and teaching that salvation is all of grace, and that man is forgiven his sins and admitted into everlasting life, solely because of what Christ has done for him, we must be careful not to exclude the most clear and emphatic teaching of Holy Scripture, that there are rewards, both in this life and the life to come, promised to good works. These rewards, however, are not of merit; but of God's free grace. No work receives a reward because it actually deserves it, but only because God has promised it. A child owes implicit obedience to his father, and merits no reward for the performance of what is only plain and simple duty. But a father may graciously attach a reward to the child's faithful performance of a duty. The boy is told that when he reaches a certain grade in his class, he shall have a book or a watch. Clear as though it is his duty to strive for this grade, without the faintest hope of reward, when the child has complied with the conditions, the reward is given, not because the child has properly earned it, but because the father has bound himself by the promise of a gracious gift. So the rewards offered by God are simply gifts of grace which He has conditioned upon the regenerate man's compliance with certain requirements.

The forgiveness of sins is no such reward. Nor is eternal life. The rewards mentioned are certain blessings within the sphere of forgiveness and eternal life, bestowed upon those who have already been gratuitously justified in Christ. No one but one who has been justified, without regard to his own merits or works, can be entitled to such rewards; since no one but one already justified, has the Holy Spirit dwelling within him, through whose influence alone such works are possible. Among the justified, therefore, there will be a difference in everlasting life, proportioned to different degrees of fidelity in this life. One star will differ from another star in glory. Some will be nearer the throne of God than others, although even the one nearest the throne will never cease to admire and praise the grace of God, which instead of casting him to the lowest Hell, has elevated him to reign with God forever. Not the least wonderful of all is it, that the Holy Spirit should work within us God's good pleasure, and then that God should reward man for what is really the fruit of the activity of the Holy Spirit, and of Christ living in man, and working through man. Thus "God crowns His own gifts within us." He bestows a gift, and then rewards us for the possession and use of this gift (Isaiah 26:12).

CHAPTER XXVII
GLORIFICATION

GLORIFYING is only the continuance of the Sanctifying Grace of the Holy Spirit. Sanctification is incipient Glorification. The transfer to Heaven will occasion far less of a break than is generally imagined. Glorification is simply another stage in the development within man of the Kingdom of God, which was implanted in Regeneration, and continued in Sanctification. While Regeneration was a purely internal, and Justification a purely external, and Sanctification both an internal and an external act of God, Glorification is the full completion of all. It entirely transforms man's character. It thoroughly delivers man from the last traces of indwelling sin. It completely restores the image of God.

But even Glorification has its degrees. The eternal world is not one of simple attainment, without the prospect of progress. When the children of God are said to "rest from their labors," it is the toil and trouble of this life that are referred to, and not the cessation of works of love, or of constant progress in ever new enjoyments of the Life Everlasting. To be absent from the body is to be present with the Lord, 2 Cor. 5:8, and to be with Christ in Paradise, Luke 23:43, and, in this presence, to be holy and unspeakably happy. But the state into which man is then ushered is one of expectancy of still greater blessings.

All the hopes and aspirations of the New Testament are directed towards the Second Coming of Christ, and the Day of Judgment. The state between death and the resurrection, unspeakably happy as it is to the regenerate, justified and sanctified children of God, and unspeakably sorrowful to those who have departed in unbelief, Luke 16:23, is only the outer court to the joys of Heaven, and the miseries of Hell. As the fallen angels are in chains reserved for judgment, Jude 5-6, and the devils look forward with anguish to their time of torment, Matt. 8:29, so faith looks forward to the resurrection of the body and the blessings promised to the soul, when there shall be restored to it the organ of its connection with the outward world, for the full consummation of its bliss.

It is at the appearing of Christ, that the children of God, seeing Him as He is, shall be made like Him, 1 John 3:2. This means both that their admission to the unobscured sight of Christ shall mark a higher stage of their transformation into His image, and also that the likeness of Christ that has already been begun in them, will give them as never before, the faculty to see and know Christ. To the latter, belongs the adage: "Some things we must know in order to love, and others we must love, in order to know." May we not expect that the believer's likeness to Christ, and his sight of Christ will act upon each other reciprocally throughout all Eternity?

With man's constantly expanding capacity to know and love and admire, there will be incessant revelations of what Christ, and of what God in Christ is; and with every new revelation, there will be the development within man of new capacities for knowing and loving and admiring. Thus, while the negative side of holiness, freedom from sin, is complete with his entrance into another world, its positive side, or the ever-increasing growth of capacities for new bestowals of grace ever advances.

The rewards in Everlasting Life are not assigned until the Day of Judgment. With death, all have entered into bliss, but the distinctions are not revealed to us, as occurring until all are judged for the things done in the body, whether they are good or bad. The Judgment Day does not settle to the child of God the question of his forgiveness, or his righteousness in Christ, but it does decide his relative position among the forgiven, as high or low, according to his use of the opportunities God has given him. They that turn many to righteousness, shall shine as the stars forever and ever, Dan. 12:3. Not until the close of the present order, and the Judgment Day, can the account of each soul be complete, since it is only then that its words and works shall cease to bring forth on earth fruit unto everlasting life. Men depart this life, but the influences they have started continue in ever-widening circles until the end of time. The lips or the fingers have crumbled to dust centuries ago, but the words they have spoken or written have been caught up by other witnesses, and make their record, for the final reckoning, in God's Book of Remembrance. Others reap the fruit in this life, but on the Judgment Day every seed that has been planted will bear its fruit to the one who has planted it.

The glorified will be endowed with resurrection bodies. These are not as ethereal, and unlike those which we have now, as is often supposed. They are not new bodies, but the very same bodies, only endowed, like our Lord's resurrection body, with new properties. It is not necessary to the identity of these bodies with those we now have, that the identity of the atoms of matter of which they are composed be maintained. As the body of the aged man is the same as that which he had in his infancy, while all its particles have been repeatedly changed, so with the resurrection body. The requisites of identity in the one case must not be made more rigid than in the other. The identity of our bodies in the present state does not lie even in the succession of particles of matter, but in the permanent impress which the soul has made upon the body, so that the body correctly expresses the soul, and continues its organ. But while this is all that is necessary for the preservation of identity, it is not for us to determine the limits of God's Omnipotence in the resurrection, or to say that God will do no more than the very least that is necessary to maintain this identity. It is enough for us to know that God will give it a body, as it pleases Him, that they that are "in their graves will hear the voice of the Son of God and shall come forth," 1 Cor. 15:38; John 5:28; Dan. 12:2, and that the body that was raised will be identical with that which was committed to the earth. These bodies will be spiritual, because freed from the dominion of sin, opposing no obstacles to the Holy Spirit, and endowed with new spiritual properties. The eye will have new capacities of sight, and the ear new capacities for hearing, and every organ be adjusted to the new sphere in which the glorified man is to move and act.

The complete annihilation of the earth has been taught upon the basis of 2 Pet. 3:12: "The heavens being on fire shall be dissolved, and the elements shall melt with fervent heat." But that this inference is not justified is clear, since it is now established that fire destroys, only by changing form and, by releasing elements from their former combinations, so as to produce new ones. The "new heavens and new earth" may mean no more than the "new heart" which is given in Sanctification. As the latter refers to the old heart endowed with new properties, so the earth itself under the fires of the Last Day, may be subjected to a change similar to that which the body of the believer will receive, so that the glorified man will live on a glorified earth. The interpretation formerly current was a mere guess, which may be true, but is not a matter of revelation.

Among the many questions connected with the glorified state, none is often fraught with more concern than that of the heavenly recognition. It is inconceivable why this should be doubted. The story of the rich man and Lazarus clearly teaches it. The immediate recognition of Moses and Elijah, while they conversed with our Lord on the Mount, shows the higher faculties for recognition with which the Apostles were endowed when raised above this earthly sphere. There is only one reason why the heavenly recognition has been doubted, and that is the apprehension that friends closely connected with us in this life may be missing, and that the knowledge of their eternal misery may disturb the happiness of the glorified. But in all this, the nature and purpose of our earthly affections are forgotten. They are implanted for purely earthly ends, in order that, to the close of his life, the wanderer may be followed by the entreaties of friends, and the prayers that God may bring him to repentance. But when the decision against God has been made with such persistency that, notwithstanding all the means which God has exerted, he dies unrepentant, God's pity for him ceases. The love that gave the Son of God to death for the wanderer's sins, is turned to eternal wrath. So in the complete Sanctification of every child of God, all purely earthly affections are removed. The glorified soul loves only what God loves, and hates all that God hates. So entirely is his will in harmony with God's will, that we cannot conceive otherwise, than that anything that God wills will be cheerfully acquiesced in. If an Apostle was willing that he himself should be accursed, in order that the progress of the Gospel might be advanced, no other calamity connected with the development of God's purposes could be regarded an evil.

They who dwell on this side of the heavenly recognition, deprive themselves of its most consolatory features. The prospect of the bliss of Heaven is increased by the anticipation of the presence of those with whom we will be reunited. There the mother will find her long-lost child; there children will rejoice in the fellowship of departed parents; there the family circle, once broken, will again be completed, except for those, for whose reclamation the utmost efforts were unavailing. There we will see at length and hold delightful intercourse with all the good and great who have preceded us. The long line of faithful witnesses to the truth, to whose efforts we owe our salvation, will be recognized and intimately known. Everyone who has brought a sinner to Christ will have his seals of rejoicing before him. There the wounds of earth will be healed, and the divisions which separated children of God on earth will be removed, and those who misunderstood and contended against one another, thoroughly united, with one heart and one mind, shall converse and celebrate the common praises of their one Lord and Master. There will be one fold and one Shepherd. All shall sit down with Abraham and Isaac and Jacob. We have a glimpse of this in Heb. 12:22-23:

> Ye are come unto Mount Zion, and unto the city of the living God, the heavenly Jerusalem, and to innumerable hosts of angels, to the General Assembly and Church of the First-Born, who are en rolled in Heaven, and to God the Judge of all, and to the spirits of just men made perfect and to Jesus the Mediator of a new covenant.

PART V
THE ADMINISTRATION OF REDEMPTION

CHAPTER XXVIII
THE CHURCH

THE doctrines of the Church and the Ministry have been reserved for the last place in this treatment, since they cannot be properly understood until we have the entire Plan of Salvation in full view, and the relations of the other doctrines to one another have been established. In the New Testament, the word, Church, occurs only three times in the Gospels, but over one hundred times in the books that succeed them.

All that has thus far been described may be summed up under the heads of Redemption, Regeneration, Justification, Sanctification, Glorification, and the Word and Sacraments as the means by which Redemption is applied, and these acts of divine grace are wrought. But in order that the Word and Sacraments may be brought to men, there is need of those who shall administer them. God neither immediately gives the means of grace (for why then, should there be means of grace?), nor does He only and sporadically and occasionally communicate them to individuals, but He has arranged a system of agencies for this purpose. It is one of the details in the vast and most complete and minute organization of His Kingdom. Everything in this Kingdom centers on Redemption, and is directed towards its saving application. For the purpose, therefore, of bringing the Word and Sacraments to men, God has instituted His Church upon earth.

Of necessity, the Church, as seen by God, and as seen by even the holiest of men, presents a very diverse form. In reality, the Church is a body composed of all who believe in Christ, in all lands and ages, organically united with one another by an unseen bond, and subordinated one to another, in working out a foreseen divine purpose. No one but He who has planned this purpose and chosen His instruments and fitted each one for His peculiar work, knows thoroughly this organism. Its unity lies in the divine mind and will. The unity of an army lies in the creative skill of its General, who has thoroughly organized, equipped and provisioned it, and causes the movement of each corps and division and brigade and regiment and company and soldier to converge upon a certain end, that may be hundreds of miles or months distant from the place and moment of present activity. The individual soldier, or even the subordinate General is probably in entire ignorance of all that pertains to any other part of the field than that which is given him to occupy. It is not for him to plan the campaign, but simply to be faithful in discharging his duty in that particular sphere which he is charged with maintaining. It is not for him to be discoursed, because of a repulse which his Commander has fore seen and determined to allow, in order to influence the ultimate issue at a remote part; or to be elated, as though the war were over, when his company has been victor in a skirmish. We see only a very small part of the field, stretching through centuries until the end of time, and encircling the whole globe. In a complicated piece of machinery, each pin and cog and rivet has its influence on the work to be done, but who can understand it until the whole be surveyed?

So the Church has been described by God. This is the thought that underlies the discussion in the Twelfth Chapter of First Corinthians, where the Church is represented as the Body of Christ, and every child of God as a member of this Body. But the members differ. They cannot all be the same, if God's purpose is to be subserved. Inherently equal, they are organically unequal. They are subordinated to one another for the attainment of the result. The body cannot be all head, or eye, or ear. Christians are members one of another. There is among them such a community of interests, that the benefit of one is the benefit of all, and the injury of one is the injury of all. Nor does this pertain only to those who are known to one another, and recognize each other as members of the same Body of Christ, but it comprehends all who belong to Christ. Each particular form of Christianity, however imperfect and defective it may appear, has its peculiar mission for the good of the whole, and of every individual belonging thereto. No gain can be made in any direction by anybody of Christians, or by any individual among them, that does not become the common gain of the entire brotherhood of Christ, now and hereafter; nor can any injury befall them, that is not co-extensive with the entire compass of the Christian Church.

The Reformers only gave prominence to this doctrine, when they taught that, in the Apostles' Creed, the clause, "the communion of saints," must be understood, as an appositive of "the Holy Christian Church," By this, they meant that the Church is not, properly speaking, the external organization, which, by a well-known figure of speech, is called by that name, but that it is the sum of all believing children of God throughout the entire world, who are united by an invisible bond. All members of this community, however separated, have common interests. No one possesses any honor or privilege as his own exclusive property, but whatever he has and is and does, pertains to the profit of the entire body of believers everywhere. No one can offer a single prayer, either for himself, or for any other member of the community, without, in this prayer, praying also for all its other members. They cannot be isolated or separated from one another. The common interests that all have are not denied or ignored, but are only enforced by defining the Church as the communion of saints.

As the edification of believers occurs through Word and Sacraments, the Church necessarily assumes an outward and visible form. It has a body as well as a soul. Wherever there is faith in Christ, it inevitably expresses itself. The faith is confessed, Rom. 10:10. But while thus, the faith is regularly and normally brought to confession, the confession of faith is often falsely made, Matt. 7:22. We cannot reverse our statement and say that, wherever there is confession, there is faith. The unbelieving are not true members of the Church, but are only externally connected with it, like the withered branches on the living vine, John 15:6. So far as their confession and teaching of the Word are correct, they are members of the Church extern ally, but not internally. All that pertains to the external side of the Church's offices, they properly perform. God's ordinances lose none of their validity, because of the inner unbelief and hypocrisy of those through whom He administers them. They act only as the hands or organs of the Church, and the Church acts only as the divinely-appointed bearer of God's never inefficacious Word and Sacraments. Even though some are false, wherever God's Word is purely preached, there are some of God's people. Although the great mass may reject it, or be hypocritical, yet some fruit is ever borne, Isaiah 55:10-11. When we say that the Church is wherever the Word is purely preached, we mean that there are always, in such assembly, some truly believing children of God.

This is what is understood when the pure preaching of the Word, and the right administration of the Sacraments are said to be the marks of the Church. The "preaching" means here the public teaching in the congregations, and otherwise through its official representatives. It is not confined to the sermons, but refers still more emphatically to the more permanent teaching, in the Church's doctrinal and devotional hand-books, in her approved journals and books, in the judgments of her theological Faculties, and carefully formulated decisions of her Synods and General Bodies. Nor is it affirmed that where the preaching is deficient in purity, it is absolutely destitute of efficacy. There are degrees of purity; and we cannot determine how small the amount of truth may be, through which God exerts His saving power. The purer the truth, however, the greater the assurance that through it truly believing children of God are born and nourished unto everlasting life. The same principle applies to the right administration of the Sacraments.

The efficacy of Word and Sacraments, as we have previously seen, is not dependent upon the correct relation of the administration to the external organization in which the Church has arranged for her work. They have an inherent efficacy both from the truth which they proclaim, and from the abiding and ever active presence within them of the Holy Spirit. It matters not what may be the instrumentality that conveys them; they are equally powerful. There may be regular and irregular ways of conveying water; but water is always water, and is quickening and refreshing however it be conveyed. The effect of the medicine is not dependent upon its prescription by a regular physician. The same prescription has precisely the same effect, even though it should come from a layman in medicine. Our Lord Himself warned His Disciples of false inferences in this particular, Luke 9:49.

But the opposite extreme must be carefully guarded against. The efficacy of the Word, even when administered in an irregular way, is no justification for carelessness and indifference concerning the regular order. Men sin in despising and breaking through a regular order, even though, notwithstanding their irregularity, their efforts may not be without marks of God's blessing. In the external regulations, connected with the preaching of His Word and the administration of His Sacraments, God has established an order, that is organized after the pattern of the invisible organization of the Church, as the Body of Christ. In this external, as well as in the internal organization, there is a sub ordination to one another of those who are in other respects equal before God. It is this order which is defined in the Fourth Commandment. Before God, as persons, the father and the child are in all respects equal; but, because of God's arrangement for carrying out His purposes in the organization of the family, they assume another relation, and the son, in obeying his father, obeys not a man who, like him, is a creature of God, redeemed by Christ, but obeys God who has instituted this order. There is every difference between the father as a man, and the father as God's agent and representative in his headship of the family.

So in the Church. A mode of organization, and form of procedure which in itself, has just as much validity and justification as another, may, because of its relations to the order which has become fixed, become wrong and sinful. Every street corner is equally holy, as a spot for the erection of a House of God; but when they to whom the decision belongs have determined upon the precise spot, the minority must have some better justification for building elsewhere than that of the equal sanctity of some other place. No organization can exist for any length of time, where there are not rules, according to which in things which are in themselves indifferent, the members agree to subordinate the exercise of their Christian liberty to the good of the whole body. These rules cannot be violated at will, but are binding upon the conscience, until there is connected with their observance the violation of some plain law of God. Even where there is no written law, the unwritten law is in force, and dare not be set aside at pleasure. While wherever two or three believers are, there is the Church, yet this gives no encouragement to the formation of an independent congregation, on the part of those who may be dissatisfied with some features of the congregation to which they have belonged. The authority inherent in the two or three believers can be claimed as a justification, only when the original organization has been used to the prejudice of the pure preaching of the Word and the right administration of the Sacraments.

We cannot reproduce in the Nineteenth Century all the details of the Church organization of the Eighteenth, Seventeenth, Sixteenth, Fifteenth Centuries, much less that of the Nicene period, or even of the Apostolic age, for the simple reason that we are not living in any other century than the Nineteenth, and that our age is very remote from that of the Apostles. We cannot, therefore, be justified in any attempt to break with a settled order, for the purpose, by purging it from post-Apostolic additions, of returning to Apostolic simplicity. This would be a denial of the presence of the Holy Spirit in the Church during the period in which He has promised in an especial way to be with it, and to lead it into all truth. The Apostolic Church was only the germ in doctrine, in life, in worship, in government, of that which was to follow. Everything that was added, in the way of true and legitimate development, is a permanent possession of the Church, which cannot be renounced, unless abused for the purpose of defeating the very end for which the Church has been organized.

Hezekiah had the courage, when the brazen serpent became an object of idolatry, to call it Nehustan, and to break it in pieces. So in the Sixteenth Century, when the organization of the Church was diverted from its proper sphere of teaching the saving doctrines of the Gospel, and the diocesan bishops refused to ordain men for the ministry in the congregations that protested against the corrupt teaching, there was no other alternative than for the congregations to claim the power that belonged to them inherently, and to repudiate the authority that repudiated God's Word. But otherwise a break with the organization which had gradually grown through the centuries, would have been wrong. A schism occurs, wherever there is a disruption of the Church's organization for any other reason, than that of notorious impurity in the teaching, that has prevailed, and that has not been remedied, after repeated and patient efforts to have it corrected. With all the emphasis we very properly place upon unity in the faith as subordinate to union in organization, we should not close our eyes to the sinfulness of schism, or attempt to justify divisions for any other cause, than for that of fidelity to our testimony to all the counsel of God. Christians are commanded to obey those who have the rule over them, and to submit themselves, Heb. 13:17, and thus there belongs to that government, which provides for spiritual things, the command to "submit yourselves to every ordinance of man for the Lord's sake," 1 Peter 2:13. The problem of Church Union will be solved only by holding firmly to the pure faith of the Gospel, once delivered to the saints, and heartily uniting with all who upon the basis of this pure faith, and for the sake of advancing this pure faith, thankfully accept and appropriate everything developed in the Church's experience, that is not contrary to God's Word. With purity of teaching guaranteed, in other respects the rule applies: "Submitting yourselves one to another in the fear of God," Eph. 5:21.

CHAPTER XXIX
THE MINISTRY

TO the Church belongs the institution of the Christian Ministry. This is not an institution above or alongside of the Church, but it is an arrangement whereby the Church is furnished with those, through whom it is to discharge the duties with which it has been entrusted. For administration, hands are always necessary. The Ministry is the Church's hands. For the power of the keys, i.e., the power to absolve from sins and to retain them, has been committed not to an order or class of men, but to the entire Church. The responsibility of providing for the administration of Word and Sacraments belongs likewise to the entire Church. This does not imply, however, that the Power of the Keys, and the administration of Word and Sacraments, belong to every member of the Church. They belong to the Church in its entirety, and then to an office, as the organ through which the Church acts.

The spiritual priesthood of all believers, and the ministerial office must always be carefully distinguished. The spiritual priesthood invests every believer with the right to approach God directly without the intervention of any other priest, but the great High Priest of our profession, the Son of God Himself, the only Mediator between God and man. It has its sacrifices to offer, but they are not propitiatory, for there is but one such, viz., the sacrifice made by Christ, once for all on the altar of the Cross, Heb. 9:28. They are Eucharistic sacrifices, the spiritual sacrifices of prayer, praise and thanksgiving, 1 Pet. 2:5; Rom. 12:1. But the Ministry is in no sense a priesthood. Hence, no argument can be derived from the spiritual priesthood to prove that the duties of the Ministry belong inherently to all the members of the Church, and that, for the sake of good order they are transferred to those set apart to this office. The Ministry does not belong to individual Christians, but to the Church in its collective capacity. The members of the Church have a voice only in deciding who shall be set apart to the office.

The voice of the people in the election of their pastor, and in the ordination of men to the Ministry by the action of their representatives, does not, however, make the minister dependent upon their will in the administration of the means of grace. He is not simply the representative of the people; he is also the representative of God, charged with the teaching of nothing but God's Word, and with the administration of the sacraments in no other way than as God has ordained. When he acts as a hand of a Christian congregation, it is only to do the work with which that congregation is charged by God. They have chosen him as their spiritual teacher. He is to declare to them all the counsel of God, whether men will hear or forbear. He dare not add anything to God's Word, or take anything from it. He must follow the written instructions, recorded in the Holy Scriptures, as rigidly as an ambassador must be guided in all things by the State Department of the government for which he acts. He must be independent of all the prejudices and influence of his people, when he applies the Word of God to any particular case, as a man, who acts upon a jury, to be true to his oath to render a verdict according to the law and the facts, must be blind to every communication which per sons in the court-room may attempt for the purpose of affecting the result. The Church has called him to the position, in which it is his constant duty to render nothing but an unprejudiced judgment. He must rebuke the erring, warn the tempted, denounce the openly wicked, and withhold the sacraments from those to whom they bring no benefit, without regard to what any member or a majority of members may say. He cannot, in this respect, transfer his responsibility even to his Church Council. The ultimate decision in the administration of the sacraments belongs not to them, but to him as their minister. Where a conflict arises, he can resign and cease to be their pastor, but he cannot perform any ministerial act which he believes is not in accordance with God's Word and will, Gal. 1:10. For should he do so, he would cease to be a minister of the Gospel, and an ambassador for Christ, 1 Cor. 4:1-3.

This does not relieve the congregation of its responsibility, or place the Ministry above the criticism of the people. The ministry must not be regarded the conscience of the laity. The minister is responsible not only to God, but to his congregation, and to all within whose fellowship he stands for the discharge of the duties of his office according to the

Word of God. The Holy Scriptures are in the hands of his people, and they are to be unwearied in the comparison of his teaching with this unerring rule, Acts 17:11. With him, they are to confer concerning aught that may seem to them inconsistent with its pure teaching. Nor are they to be silent, when after repeated conversations, they find his teaching unscriptural. There is always a regular order of procedure by which such faults may be remedied. But, notwithstanding this, as long as he remains pastor, the responsibility for what is taught, and for the right administration of the sacraments remains with him.

All ministers are intrinsically equal. The parity of ministers rests upon the fact that all are equally entrusted with the same Word and the same sacraments, whose administration is equally accompanied by the Holy Spirit. This, however, does not interfere with the subordination of one to the other for the sake of expediency in the more comprehensive spheres of Church organization. One can readily become in this way, *primus inter pares*, the first among equals. While, therefore, the teaching that there are different orders in the Ministry by divine right, is incorrect, such orders by human right, would not be wrong in the Church, but must occur wherever the organization of the Church to any great extent occurs. Organization, the Church, as a human society, must have, and such organization implies the existence of diverse offices. The New Testament bishops and presbyters or elders, according to the acknowledgement of even decided advocates of diocesan episcopacy, are entirely synonymous. But the subsequent diocesan episcopacy, with the theory of Apostolic succession eliminated, lies at the basis of forms of Church organization perfectly in harmony with New Testament principles. Of these, some are episcopal in fact, but not in name. Its only rival in any extended scheme of organization, is the Presbyterian, which, however, is scarcely more than an undeveloped form of an Episcopacy, that does not proceed beyond the limits prescribed in the New Testament.

All power in the Church being that of the Word and sacraments, it is entirely without jurisdiction in secular affairs. It can impose no other than purely spiritual penalties. Nevertheless as the Church, in carrying on her divinely-given work, cannot dispense with secular arrangements, she has to deal with secularities. In this lies the danger of her secularization. The array of numbers, of contributions, of property, of perfection of organization, etc., may often be interpreted as an evidence of spirituality, while, on the other hand, it may only hide a very lamentable degree of spiritual poverty. The Church is strong, as it confesses clearly, plainly and unwaveringly the whole Word of God; it is weak, as it places reliance upon any other means than this for conquering the world.

The Church has a varied lot in this world; but there is no danger, that it will ever become extinct. The promise is that however threatening the assaults of her enemies, "God is in her midst; she shall not be moved. God shall help her and that right early," Ps. 46:5. Built upon a rock, "the gates of Hell shall not prevail against it," Matt. 16:18. The Gospel is to be preached among all nations, and to every creature; and wherever the Gospel is preached, baptism is to attend it. The Lord's Supper is to be administered until Christ's return, 1 Cor. 11:26. In alternate light and shade, the Church advances towards its final triumph. The good and the evil grow together until the end, the good becoming better, and the evil worse. Every now and then, an hour of conflict comes, and the blood of martyrs flows. The result is always a victory, but not permanent peace. Every out-breaking error and heresy precipitates a controversy, and a new gain for the Church. Yet the goal is not here, but beyond. The believing child of the Church is not indifferent to its future on the earth. He does all he can for its prosperity while he lives here, and for its perpetuity and diffusion after he has gone. But beyond this, he rejoices from afar in the clear vision, granted faith, of the Church Triumphant. Upon these his thoughts dwell, and towards them all his aspirations turn. For his citizenship is in Heaven. In the Church Triumphant, the Kingdom of God attains its ultimate goal. Redemption then will be not only fully appropriated by believers, but appropriated Redemption will be completely actualized.

> The tabernacle of God is with men, and He will dwell with them, and they shall be His people, and God Himself shall be with them, and be their God. And God shall wipe away all tears from their eyes; and there shall be no more death, neither sorrow, nor crying, neither shall there be any more pain: for the former things are passed away. (Rev. 21:3-4)

Made in the USA
Charleston, SC
26 November 2014